CITIES

CITIES

a
**SCIENTIFIC
AMERICAN**
book

NEW YORK: ALFRED·A·KNOPF

1971

L. C. catalog card number: 65-28177

THIS IS A BORZOI BOOK,
PUBLISHED BY ALFRED A. KNOPF, INC.

Published November 15, 1965
Thirteenth Printing, April 1971

*The twelve chapters in this book originally ap-
peared as articles in the September 1965 issue of
Scientific American.*

Introduction

"I LIKE not the town. Think'st thou, Pierre, the time will ever come when all the earth shall be paved?"

"Thank God, that can never be!" Herman Melville's Pierre replied. Yet the time is coming soon when most people will live in cities. Already 70 percent of the citizens of the United States and comparable percentages of the people of other industrial countries have become city dwellers. And half of the cities on any list of the world's largest cities, it turns out, are located in the underdeveloped countries. If the process of urbanization continues at its present rate, the majority of the world population will be gathered in cities of 100,000 or more at the end of the present century.

The authors of this book reckon with nothing less than the opening of a new phase in human evolution. "The large and dense agglomerations comprising the urban population," says Kingsley Davis in the first chapter, ". . . exceed in size the communities of any other large animal; they suggest the behavior of communal insects rather than of mammals." The city dweller of today needs to be reminded that only a small, socially dominant minority lived in the cities of the pre-industrial civilized world. In the urban industrial societies, cities are the primary centers of human occupation; agriculture accounts for no more than 5 percent of the gross national product of the United States. The industrial revolution has committed mankind to existence in what Hans Blumenfeld calls a "basically new form of human settlement."

Four cities on different continents indicate in this book the diversity of the new form of human settlement. They illustrate in different ways how far men have failed to make their cities fit for human habitation. The story of each city shows how the builders of the city of man must recognize that the city is already in the possession of living men. The same lesson is drawn by the next four articles that examine paradoxes of scarcity and plenty: the shortage of city land in the United States, for example, where city dwellers occupy only .7 percent of the land; the scarcity of potable water and fresh air on the only planet that offers either in abundance; the increase in travel time with increase in mobility; the decrease in dwelling units with increase in public expenditure for housing. Plainly the generosity of nature and human ingenuity hold out ready solutions for these and other problems of urban life. The question that needs to be answered is posed by Kevin Lynch in the last chapter: "Imagine that the growth of population and the evolution of technology have urbanized the entire globe— that a single world city covers the usable surface of the earth. . . . What could we do to make it a more human place?"

The chapters of this book made up the content of a single-topic issue of *Scientific American* published in September 1965. As indicated by the recent act of Congress establishing a Department of Urban Affairs in the cabinet of the President of the United States, the subject of this issue holds interest for readers far beyond the magazine's regular monthly circulation of 400,000. The editors of *Scientific American* therefore thank their colleagues at Alfred A. Knopf for so speedily extending the circulation of *Cities* and the life of this issue of the magazine in book form.

September 1965   THE EDITORS *

* BOARD OF EDITORS: Gerard Piel (Publisher), Dennis Flanagan (Editor), Francis Bello (Associate Editor), Frederick H. Gardner, James R. Newman, John Purcell, James T. Rogers, Armand Schwab, Jr., C. L. Stong, Joseph Wisnovsky.

Contents

List of Illustrations

CITIES

The Urbanization of the Human Population

· KINGSLEY DAVIS

This introductory chapter outlines how cities arose, how they are evolving in various circumstances, and how they shape themselves. More than half of the world's people will probably be living in cities of 100,000 or more by 1990.

URBANIZED SOCIETIES, in which a majority of the people live crowded together in towns and cities, represent a new and fundamental step in man's social evolution. Although cities themselves first appeared some 5,500 years ago, they were small and surrounded by an overwhelming majority of rural people; moreover, they relapsed easily to village or small-town status. The urbanized societies of today, in contrast, not only have urban agglomerations of a size never before attained but also have a high proportion of their population concentrated in such agglomerations. In 1960, for example, nearly 52 million Americans lived in only 16 urbanized areas. Together these areas covered less land than one of the smaller counties (Cochise) of Arizona. According to one definition used by the U.S. Bureau of the Census, 96 million people—53 percent of the nation's population—were concentrated in 213 urbanized areas that together occupied only .7 percent of the nation's land. Another definition used by the bureau puts the

urban population at about 70 percent. The large and dense agglomerations comprising the urban population involve a degree of
human contact and of social complexity never before known.
They exceed in size the communities of any other large animal;
they suggest the behavior of communal insects rather than of
mammals.

Neither the recency nor the speed of this evolutionary development is widely appreciated. Before 1850 no society could be described as predominantly urbanized, and by 1900 only one—Great
Britain—could be so regarded. Today, only 65 years later, all industrial nations are highly urbanized, and in the world as a whole
the process of urbanization is accelerating rapidly.

Some years ago my associates and I at Columbia University
undertook to document the progress of urbanization by compil-
ing data on the world's cities and the proportion of human beings
living in them; in recent years the work has been continued in our
center—International Population and Urban Research—at the University of California at Berkeley. The data obtained in these investigations can be used to show the historical trend in terms of
one index of urbanization: the proportion of the population living
in cities of 100,000 or larger. Statistics of this kind are only approximations of reality, but they are accurate enough to demonstrate how urbanization has accelerated. Between 1850 and 1950
the index changed at a much higher rate than from 1800 to 1850,
but the rate of change from 1950 to 1960 was twice that of the
preceding 50 years! If the pace of increase that obtained between
1950 and 1960 were to remain the same, by 1990 the fraction of the
world's people living in cities of 100,000 or larger would be more
than half. Using another index of urbanization—the proportion of
the world's population living in urban places of all sizes—we found
that by 1960 the figure had already reached 33 percent.

Clearly the world as a whole is not fully urbanized, but it soon
will be. This change in human life is so recent that even the most
urbanized countries still exhibit the rural origins of their institutions. Its full implications for man's organic and social evolution
can only be surmised.

In discussing the trend—and its implications insofar as they can
be perceived—I shall use the term "urbanization" in a particular
way. It refers here to the proportion of the total population con-

centrated in urban settlements, or else to a rise in this proportion. A common mistake is to think of urbanization as simply the growth of cities. Since the total population is composed of both the urban population and the rural, however, the "proportion urban" is a function of both of them. Accordingly cities can grow without any urbanization, provided that the rural population grows at an equal or a greater rate.

Historically urbanization and the growth of cities have occurred together, which accounts for the confusion. As the reader will soon see, it is necessary to distinguish the two trends. In the most advanced countries today, for example, urban populations are still growing, but their proportion of the total population is tending to remain stable or to diminish. In other words, the process of urbanization—the switch from a spread-out pattern of human settlement to one of concentration in urban centers—is a change that has a beginning and an end, but the growth of cities has no inherent limit. Such growth could continue even after everyone was living in cities, through sheer excess of births over deaths.

The difference between a rural village and an urban community is of course one of degree; a precise operational distinction is somewhat arbitrary, and it varies from one nation to another. Since data are available for communities of various sizes, a dividing line can be chosen at will. One convenient index of urbanization, for example, is the proportion of people living in places of 100,000 or more. In the following analysis I shall depend on two indexes: the one just mentioned and the proportion of population classed as "urban" in the official statistics of each country. In practice the two indexes are highly correlated; therefore either one can be used as an index of urbanization.

Actually the hardest problem is not that of determining the "floor" of the urban category but of ascertaining the boundary of places that are clearly urban by any definition. How far east is the boundary of Los Angeles? Where along the Hooghly River does Calcutta leave off and the countryside begin? In the past the population of cities and towns has usually been given as the number of people living within the political boundaries. Thus the population of New York is frequently given as around eight million, this being the population of the city proper. The error in such a figure was not large before World War I, but since then, particularly in the advanced countries, urban populations have been spilling over the narrow political boundaries at a tremendous rate. In 1960 the New York–Northeastern New Jersey urbanized area, as delineated by the Bureau of the Census, had more than 14 million people. That delineation showed it to be the largest city in the world and nearly twice as large as New York City proper.

As a result of the outward spread of urbanites, counts made on the basis of political boundaries alone underestimate the city populations and exaggerate the rural. For this reason our office delineated the metropolitan areas of as many countries as possible for dates around 1950. These areas included the central, or political, cities and the zones around them that are receiving the spillover.

This reassessment raised the estimated proportion of the world's population in cities of 100,000 or larger from 15.1 percent to 16.7 percent. As of 1960 we have used wherever possible the "urban agglomeration" data now furnished to the United Nations by many countries. The U.S., for example, provides data for "urbanized areas," meaning cities of 50,000 or larger and the built-up agglomerations around them.

The origin and evolution of cities is discussed by Gideon Sjoberg in the next chapter. My concern is with the degree of urbanization in whole societies. It is curious that thousands of years elapsed between the first appearance of small cities and the emergence of urbanized societies in the 19th century. It is also curious that the region where urbanized societies arose—northwestern Europe— was not the one that had given rise to the major cities of the past; on the contrary, it was a region where urbanization had been at an extremely low ebb. Indeed, the societies of northwestern Europe in medieval times were so rural that it is hard for modern minds to comprehend them. Perhaps it was the nonurban character of these societies that erased the parasitic nature of towns and eventually provided a new basis for a revolutionary degree of urbanization.

At any rate, two seemingly adverse conditions may have presaged the age to come: one the low productivity of medieval agriculture in both per-acre and per-man terms, the other the feudal social system. The first meant that towns could not prosper on the

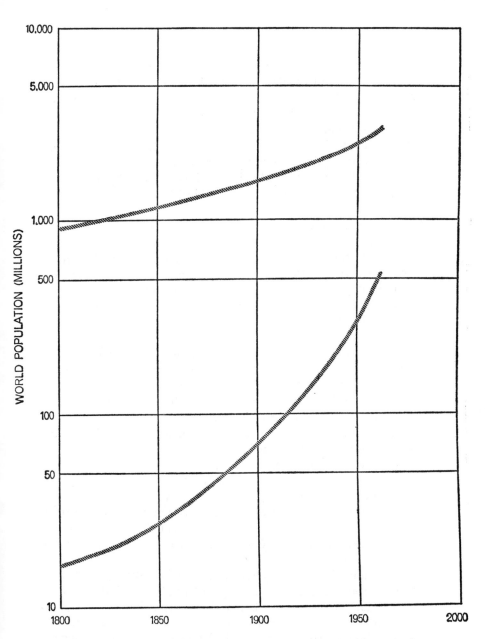

RAPID URBANIZATION of the world's population is evident in this comparison of total population (upper curve) with the population in cities of more than 100,000 inhabitants (lower curve) over more than a century and a half. The use of cities of 100,000 or larger to define an urban population shows a close correlation with other definitions of urbanism.

basis of local agriculture alone but had to trade and to manufacture something to trade. The second meant that they could not
gain political dominance over their hinterlands and thus become
warring city-states. Hence they specialized in commerce and
manufacture and evolved local institutions suited to this role.
Craftsmen were housed in the towns, because there the merchants
could regulate quality and cost. Competition among towns stimulated specialization and technological innovation. The need for
literacy, accounting skills and geographical knowledge caused the
towns to invest in secular education.

Although the medieval towns remained small and never embraced more than a minor fraction of each region's population, the
close connection between industry and commerce that they fostered, together with their emphasis on technique, set the stage for
the ultimate breakthrough in urbanization. This breakthrough
came only with the enormous growth in productivity caused by
the use of inanimate energy and machinery. How difficult it was to
achieve the transition is agonizingly apparent from statistics show-
ing that even with the conquest of the New World the growth
of urbanization during three postmedieval centuries in Europe was
barely perceptible. I have assembled population estimates at two
or more dates for 33 towns and cities in the 16th century, 46 in
the 17th and 61 in the 18th. The average rate of growth during
the three centuries was less than .6 percent per year. Estimates of
the growth of Europe's population as a whole between 1650 and
1800 work out to slightly more than .4 percent. The advantage
of the towns was evidently very slight. Taking only the cities of
100,000 or more inhabitants, one finds that in 1600 their combined
population was 1.6 percent of the estimated population of Europe;
in 1700, 1.9 percent, and in 1800, 2.2 percent. On the eve of the
industrial revolution Europe was still an overwhelmingly agrarian
region.

With industrialization, however, the transformation was striking.
By 1801 nearly a tenth of the people of England and Wales were
living in cities of 100,000 or larger. This proportion doubled in 40
years and doubled again in another 60 years. By 1900 Britain was
an urbanized society. In general, the later each country became industrialized, the faster was its urbanization. The change from a
population with 10 percent of its members in cities of 100,000 or

larger to one in which 30 percent lived in such cities took about 79 years in England and Wales, 66 in the U.S., 48 in Germany, 36 in Japan and 26 in Australia. The close association between economic development and urbanization has persisted; in 199 countries around 1960 the proportion of the population living in cities varied sharply with per capita income.

Clearly modern urbanization is best understood in terms of its connection with economic growth, and its implications are best perceived in its latest manifestations in advanced countries. What becomes apparent as one examines the trend in these countries is that urbanization is a finite process, a cycle through which nations go in their transition from agrarian to industrial society. The intensive urbanization of most of the advanced countries began within the past 100 years; in the underdeveloped countries it got under way more recently. In some of the advanced countries its end is now in sight. The fact that it will end, however, does not mean that either economic development or the growth of cities will necessarily end.

The typical cycle of urbanization can be represented by a curve in the shape of an attenuated S. Starting from the bottom of the S, the first bend tends to come early and to be followed by a long attenuation. In the United Kingdom, for instance, the swiftest rise in the proportion of people living in cities of 100,000 or larger occurred from 1811 to 1851. In the U.S. it occurred from 1820 to 1890, in Greece from 1879 to 1921. As the proportion climbs above 50 percent the curve begins to flatten out; it falters, or even declines, when the proportion urban has reached about 75 percent. In the United Kingdom, one of the world's most urban countries, the proportion was slightly higher in 1926 (78.7 percent) than in 1961 (78.3 percent).

At the end of the curve some ambiguity appears. As a society becomes advanced enough to be highly urbanized it can also afford considerable suburbanization and fringe development. In a sense the slowing down of urbanization is thus more apparent than real: an increasing proportion of urbanites simply live in the country and are classified as rural. Many countries now try to compensate for this ambiguity by enlarging the boundaries of urban places; they did so in numerous censuses taken around 1960. Whether in these cases the old classification of urban or the new one is errone-

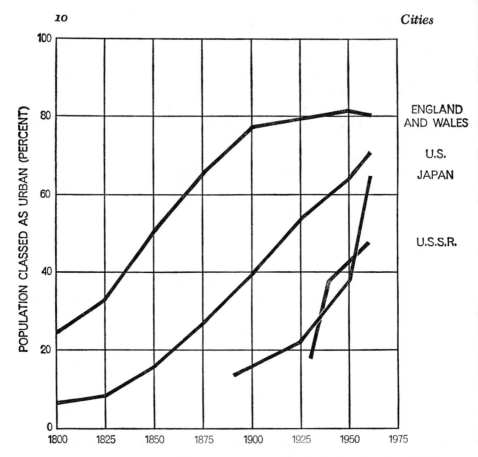

INDUSTRIALIZED NATIONS underwent a process of urbanization that is typified by the curves shown here for four countries. It was closely related to economic development. The figures for 1950 and 1960 are based on a classification that counts as urban the fringe residents of urbanized areas; that classification was not used for the earlier years shown.

ous depends on how one looks at it; at a very advanced stage the entire concept of urbanization becomes ambiguous.

The end of urbanization cannot be unraveled without going into the ways in which economic development governs urbanization. Here the first question is: Where do the urbanites come from? The possible answers are few: The proportion of people in cities can rise because rural settlements grow larger and are

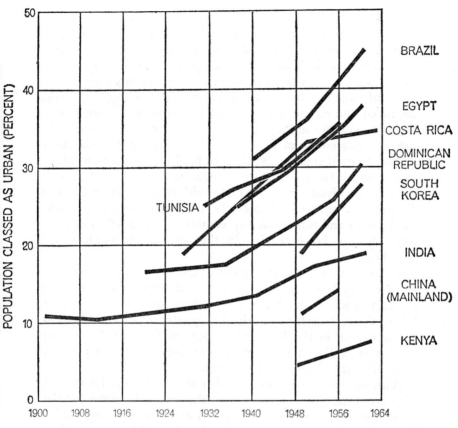

NONINDUSTRIAL NATIONS are undergoing a process of urbanization that is typified by these curves. The process started much later than in the industrialized nations, as can be seen by comparing this chart with the one on page 10, and is attributable more to the rapid rise of total population in these countries than to economic development.

reclassified as towns or cities; because the excess of births over deaths is greater in the city than in the country, or because people move from the country to the city.

The first factor has usually had only slight influence. The second has apparently never been the case. Indeed, a chief obstacle to the growth of cities in the past has been their excessive mortality. London's water in the middle of the 19th century came mainly from wells and rivers that drained cesspools, graveyards and tidal areas. The city was regularly ravaged by cholera. Tables for 1841 show an expectation of life of about 36 years for London and 26 for Liverpool and Manchester, as compared to 41 for England and Wales as a whole. After 1850, mainly as a result of sanitary measures and some improvement in nutrition and housing, city health improved, but as late as the period 1901–1910 the death rate of the urban counties in England and Wales, as modified to make the age structure comparable, was 33 percent higher than the death rate of the rural counties. As Bernard Benjamin, a chief statistician of the British General Register Office, has remarked: "Living in the town involved not only a higher risk of epidemic and crowd diseases . . . but also a higher risk of degenerative disease—the harder wear and tear of factory employment and urban discomfort." By 1950, however, virtually the entire differential had been wiped out.

As for birth rates, during rapid urbanization in the past they were notably lower in cities than in rural areas. In fact, the gap tended to widen somewhat as urbanization proceeded in the latter half of the 19th century and the first quarter of the 20th. In 1800 urban women in the U.S. had 36 percent fewer children than rural women did; in 1840, 38 percent and in 1930, 41 percent. Thereafter the difference diminished.

With mortality in the cities higher and birth rates lower, and with reclassification a minor factor, the only real source for the growth in the proportion of people in urban areas during the industrial transition was rural-urban migration. This source had to be plentiful enough not only to overcome the substantial disadvantage of the cities in natural increase but also, above that, to furnish a big margin of growth in their populations. If, for example, the cities had a death rate a third higher and a birth rate a third lower than the rural rates (as was typical in the latter half of the 19th century), they would require each year perhaps 40 to 45 migrants from elsewhere per 1,000 of their population to maintain a growth rate of 3 percent per year. Such a rate of migration could easily be maintained as long as the rural portion of the population was large, but when this condition ceased to obtain, the maintenance of the same urban rate meant an increasing drain on the countryside.

Why did the rural-urban migration occur? The reason was that the rise in technological enhancement of human productivity, together with certain constant factors, rewarded urban concentration. One of the constant factors was that agriculture uses land as its prime instrument of production and hence spreads out people who are engaged in it, whereas manufacturing, commerce and services use land only as a site. Moreover, the demand for agricultural products is less elastic than the demand for services and manufactures. As productivity grows, services and manufactures can absorb more manpower by paying higher wages. Since nonagricultural activities can use land simply as a site, they can locate near one another (in towns and cities) and thus minimize the friction of space inevitably involved in the division of labor. At the same time, as agricultural technology is improved, capital costs in farming rise and manpower becomes not only less needed but also economically more burdensome. A substantial portion of the agricultural population is therefore sufficiently disadvantaged, in relative terms, to be attracted by higher wages in other sectors.

In this light one sees why a large flow of people from farms to cities was generated in every country that passed through the industrial revolution. One also sees why, with an even higher proportion of people already in cities and with the inability of city people to replace themselves by reproduction, the drain eventually became so heavy that in many nations the rural population began to decline in absolute as well as relative terms. In Sweden it declined after 1920, in England and Wales after 1861, in Belgium after 1910.

Realizing that urbanization is transitional and finite, one comes on another fact—a fact that throws light on the circumstances in which urbanization comes to an end. A basic feature of the transition is the profound switch from agricultural to nonagricultural employment. This change is associated with urbanization but not identical with it. The difference emerges particularly in the later stages. Then the availability of automobiles, radios, motion pictures and electricity, as well as the reduction of the workweek and the workday, mitigate the disadvantages of living in the country. Concurrently the expanding size of cities makes them more difficult to live in. The population classed as "rural" is accordingly enlarged, both from cities and from true farms.

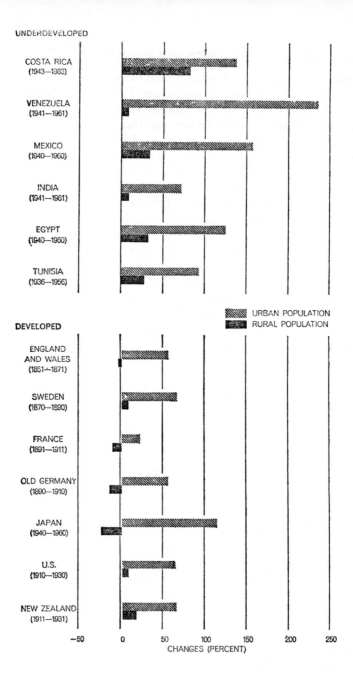

RURAL AND URBAN POPULATIONS of several undeveloped countries are compared with those in the currently developed countries at a time when they were undergoing rapid urbanization. It is evident that in the underdeveloped countries the rural population is rising in spite of urbanization, whereas in the earlier period it rose slightly or dropped.

For these reasons the "rural" population in some industrial countries never did fall in absolute size. In all the industrial countries,
however, the population dependent on agriculture—which the
reader will recognize as a more functional definition of the nonurban population than mere rural residence—decreased in absolute as well as relative terms. In the U.S., for example, the net
migration from farms totaled more than 27 million between 1920
and 1959 and thus averaged approximately 700,000 a year. As a
result the farm population declined from 32.5 million in 1916 to
20.5 million in 1960, in spite of the large excess of births in farm
families. In 1964, by a stricter American definition classifying as
"farm families" only those families actually earning their living
from agriculture, the farm population was down to 12.9 million.
This number represented 6.8 percent of the nation's population;
the comparable figure for 1880 was 44 percent. In Great Britain
the number of males occupied in agriculture was at its peak, 1.8
million, in 1851; by 1961 it had fallen to .5 million.

In the later stages of the cycle, then, urbanization in the industrial countries tends to cease. Hence the connection between
economic development and the growth of cities also ceases. The
change is explained by two circumstances. First, there is no longer
enough farm population to furnish a significant migration to the
cities. (What can 12.9 million American farmers contribute to
the growth of the 100 million people already in urbanized areas?)
Second, the rural nonfarm population, nourished by refugees from
the expanding cities, begins to increase as fast as the city population.
The effort of census bureaus to count fringe residents as urban
simply pushes the definition of "urban" away from the notion of
dense settlement and in the direction of the term "nonfarm." As
the urban population becomes more "rural," which is to say less
densely settled, the advanced industrial peoples are for a time able
to enjoy the amenities of urban life without the excessive crowding of the past.

Here, however, one again encounters the fact that a cessation
of urbanization does not necessarily mean a cessation of city
growth. An example is provided by New Zealand. Between 1945
and 1961 the proportion of New Zealand's population classed as
urban—that is, the ratio between urban and rural residents—
changed hardly at all (from 61.3 percent to 63.6 percent) but the

urban population increased by 50 percent. In Japan between 1940 and 1950 urbanization actually decreased slightly, but the urban population increased by 13 percent.

The point to be kept in mind is that once urbanization ceases, city growth becomes a function of general population growth. Enough farm-to-city migration may still occur to redress the difference in natural increase. The reproductive rate of urbanites tends, however, to increase when they live at lower densities, and the reproductive rate of "urbanized" farmers tends to decrease; hence little migration is required to make the urban increase equal the national increase.

I now turn to the currently underdeveloped countries. With the advanced nations having slackened their rate of urbanization, it is the others—representing three-fourths of humanity—that are mainly responsible for the rapid urbanization now characterizing the world as a whole. In fact, between 1950 and 1960 the proportion of the population in cities of 100,000 or more rose about a third faster in the underdeveloped regions than in the developed ones. Among the underdeveloped regions the pace was slow in eastern and southern Europe, but in the rest of the underdeveloped world the proportion in cities rose twice as fast as it did in the industrialized countries, even though the latter countries in many cases broadened their definitions of urban places to include more suburban and fringe residents.

Because of the characteristic pattern of urbanization, the current rates of urbanization in underdeveloped countries could be expected to exceed those now existing in countries far advanced in the cycle. On discovering that this is the case one is tempted to say that the underdeveloped regions are now in the typical stage of urbanization associated with early economic development. This notion, however, is erroneous. In their urbanization the underdeveloped countries are definitely not repeating past history. Indeed, the best grasp of their present situation comes from analyzing how their course differs from the previous pattern of development.

The first thing to note is that today's underdeveloped countries are urbanizing not only more rapidly than the industrial nations are now but also more rapidly than the industrial nations did in the heyday of their urban growth. The difference, however, is not large. In 40 underdeveloped countries for which we have data in recent decades, the average gain in the proportion of the population urban was 20 percent per decade; in 16 industrial countries, during the decades of their most rapid urbanization (mainly in the 19th century), the average gain per decade was 15 percent.

This finding that urbanization is proceeding only a little faster in underdeveloped countries than it did historically in the advanced nations may be questioned by the reader. It seemingly belies the widespread impression that cities throughout the nonindustrial parts of the world are bursting with people. There is, however, no contradiction. One must recall the basic distinction between a change in the proportion of the population urban, which is a ratio, and the absolute growth of cities. The popular impression is correct: the cities in underdeveloped areas are growing at a disconcerting rate. They are far outstripping the city boom of the industrializing era in the 19th century. If they continue their recent rate of growth, they will double their population every 15 years.

In 34 underdeveloped countries for which we have data relating to the 1940's and 1950's, the average annual gain in the urban population was 4.5 percent. The figure is remarkably similar for the various regions: 4.7 percent in seven countries of Africa, 4.7 percent in 15 countries of Asia and 4.3 percent in 12 countries of Latin America. In contrast, in nine European countries during their period of fastest urban population growth (mostly in the latter half of the 19th century) the average gain per year was 2.1 percent. Even the frontier industrial countries—the U.S., Australia–New Zealand, Canada and Argentina—which received huge numbers of immigrants, had a smaller population growth in towns and cities: 4.2 percent per year. In Japan and the U.S.S.R. the rate was respectively 5.4 and 4.3 percent per year, but their economic growth began only recently.

How is it possible that the contrast in growth between today's underdeveloped countries and yesterday's industrializing countries is sharper with respect to the absolute urban population than with respect to the urban share of the total population? The answer lies in another profound difference between the two sets of countries—a difference in total population growth, rural as well as urban. Contemporary underdeveloped populations have been growing since 1940 more than twice as fast as industrialized populations, and their increase far exceeds the growth of the latter at the peak of their expansion. The only rivals in an earlier day were the frontier nations, which had the help of great streams of immigrants. Today the underdeveloped nations—already densely settled, tragically impoverished and with gloomy economic prospects—are multiplying their people by sheer biological increase at a rate that is unprecedented. It is this population boom that is overwhelmingly responsible for the rapid inflation of city populations in such countries. Contrary to popular opinion both inside and outside those countries, the main factor is not rural-urban migration.

This point can be demonstrated easily by a calculation that has the effect of eliminating the influence of general population growth on urban growth. The calculation involves assuming that the total population of a given country remained constant over a period of time but that the percentage urban changed as it did historically. In this manner one obtains the growth of the absolute urban population that would have occurred if rural-urban migration were the only factor affecting it. As an example, Costa Rica had in 1927 a total population of 471,500, of which 88,600, or 18.8 percent, was urban. By 1963 the country's total population was 1,325,200 and the urban population was 456,600, or 34.5 percent. If the total population had remained at 471,500 but the percentage urban had still risen from 18.8 to 34.5, the absolute urban population in 1963 would have been only 162,700. That is the growth that would have occurred in the urban population if rural-urban migration had been the only factor. In actuality the urban population rose to 456,600. In other words, only 20 percent of the rapid growth of Costa Rica's towns and cities was attributable to urbanization per se; 44 percent was attributable solely to the country's general population increase, the remainder to the joint operation of both factors. Similarly, in Mexico between 1940 and 1960, 50 percent of the urban population increase was attributable to national multiplication alone and only 22 percent to urbanization alone.

The past performance of the advanced countries presents a sharp contrast. In Switzerland between 1850 and 1888, when the proportion urban resembled that in Costa Rica recently, general population growth alone accounted for only 19 percent of the increase of town and city people, and rural-urban migration alone accounted for 69 percent. In France between 1846 and 1911 only 21 percent of the growth in the absolute urban population was due to general growth alone.

The conclusion to which this contrast points is that one anxiety of governments in the underdeveloped nations is misplaced. Impressed by the mushrooming in their cities of shantytowns filled with ragged peasants, they attribute the fantastically fast city growth to rural-urban migration. Actually this migration now does little more than make up for the small difference in the birth rate between city and countryside. In the history of the industrial nations, as we have seen, the sizable difference between urban and rural birth rates and death rates required that cities, if they were to grow, had to have an enormous influx of people from farms and villages. Today in the underdeveloped countries the towns and cities have only a slight disadvantage in fertility, and their old disadvantage in mortality not only has been wiped out but also in many cases has been reversed. During the 19th century the urbanizing nations were learning how to keep crowded populations in cities from dying like flies. Now the lesson has been learned, and it is being applied to cities even in countries just emerging from tribalism. In fact, a disproportionate share of public health funds goes into cities. As a result throughout the nonindustrial world people in cities are multiplying as never before, and rural-urban migration is playing a much lesser role.

The trends just described have an important implication for the rural population. Given the explosive overall population growth in underdeveloped countries, it follows that if the rural population is not to pile up on the land and reach an economically absurd density, a high rate of rural-urban migration must be maintained. Indeed, the exodus from rural areas should be higher than in the past. But this high rate of internal movement is not taking place, and there is some doubt that it could conceivably do so.

To elaborate I shall return to my earlier point that in the evolution of industrialized countries the rural citizenry often declined in absolute as well as relative terms. The rural population

of France—26.8 million in 1846—was down to 20.8 million by
1926 and 17.2 million by 1962, notwithstanding a gain in the
nation's total population during this period. Sweden's rural population dropped from 4.3 million in 1910 to 3.5 million in 1960.
Since the category "rural" includes an increasing portion of
urbanites living in fringe areas, the historical drop was more
drastic and consistent specifically in the farm population. In the
U.S., although the "rural" population never quite ceased to grow,
the farm contingent began its long descent shortly after the turn
of the century; today it is less than two-fifths of what it was
in 1910.

   This transformation is not occurring in contemporary underdeveloped countries. In spite of the enormous growth of their
cities, their rural populations—and their more narrowly defined
agricultural populations—are growing at a rate that in many cases
exceeds the rise of even the urban population during the evolution of the now advanced countries. The poor countries thus
confront a grave dilemma. If they do not substantially step up
the exodus from rural areas, these areas will be swamped with
underemployed farmers. If they do step up the exodus, the cities
will grow at a disastrous rate.

   The rapid growth of cities in the advanced countries, painful
though it was, had the effect of solving a problem—the problem
of the rural population. The growth of cities enabled agricultural
holdings to be consolidated, allowed increased capitalization and
in general resulted in greater efficiency. Now, however, the
underdeveloped countries are experiencing an even more rapid
urban growth—and are suffering from urban problems—but urbanization is not solving their rural ills.

   A case in point is Venezuela. Its capital, Caracas, jumped from
a population of 359,000 in 1941 to 1,507,000 in 1963; other Venezuelan towns and cities equaled or exceeded this growth. Is this
rapid rise denuding the countryside of people? No, the Venezuelan farm population increased in the decade 1951–1961 by 11
percent. The only thing that declined was the amount of cultivated land. As a result the agricultural population density became
worse. In 1950 there were some 64 males engaged in agriculture
per square mile of cultivated land; in 1961 there were 78. (Compare this with 4.8 males occupied in agriculture per square mile

of cultivated land in Canada, 6.8 in the U.S. and 15.6 in Argentina.) With each male occupied in agriculture there are of course dependents. Approximately 225 persons in Venezuela are trying to live from each square mile of cultivated land. Most of the growth of cities in Venezuela is attributable to overall population growth. If the general population had not grown at all, and internal migration had been large enough to produce the actual shift in the proportion in cities, the increase in urban population would have been only 28 percent of what it was and the rural population would have been reduced by 57 percent.

The story of Venezuela is being repeated virtually everywhere in the underdeveloped world. It is not only Caracas that has thousands of squatters living in self-constructed junk houses on land that does not belong to them. By whatever name they are called, the squatters are to be found in all major cities in the poorer countries. They live in broad gullies beneath the main plain in San Salvador and on the hillsides of Rio de Janeiro and Bogotá. They tend to occupy with implacable determination parks, school grounds and vacant lots. Amman, the capital of Jordan, grew from 12,000 in 1958 to 247,000 in 1961. A good part of it is slums, and urban amenities are lacking most of the time for most of the people. Greater Baghdad now has an estimated 850,000 people; its slums, like those in many other underdeveloped countries, are in two zones—the central part of the city and the outlying areas. Here are the *sarifa* areas, characterized by self-built reed huts; these areas account for about 45 percent of the housing in the entire city and are devoid of amenities, including even latrines. In addition to such urban problems, all the countries struggling for higher living levels find their rural population growing too and piling up on already crowded land.

I have characterized urbanization as a transformation that, unlike economic development, is finally accomplished and comes to an end. At the 1950–1960 rate the term "urbanized world" will be applicable well before the end of the century. One should scarcely expect, however, that mankind will complete its urbanization without major complications. One sign of trouble ahead turns on the distinction I made at the start between urbanization and city growth per se. Around the globe today city growth is disproportionate to urbanization. The discrepancy is paradoxical in the industrial nations and worse than paradoxical in the non-industrial.

It is in this respect that the nonindustrial nations, which still make up the great majority of nations, are far from repeating past history. In the 19th and early 20th centuries the growth of cities arose from and contributed to economic advancement. Cities took surplus manpower from the countryside and put it to work producing goods and services that in turn helped to modernize agriculture. But today in underdeveloped countries, as in present-day advanced nations, city growth has become increasingly unhinged from economic development and hence from rural-urban migration. It derives in greater degree from overall population growth, and this growth in nonindustrial lands has become unprecedented because of modern health techniques combined with high birth rates.

The speed of world population growth is twice what it was before 1940, and the swiftest increase has shifted from the advanced to the backward nations. In the latter countries, consequently, it is virtually impossible to create city services fast enough to take care of the huge, never-ending cohorts of babies and peasants swelling the urban masses. It is even harder to expand agricultural land and capital fast enough to accommodate the enormous natural increase on farms. The problem is not urbanization, not rural-urban migration, but human multiplication. It is a problem that is new in both its scale and its setting, and runaway city growth is only one of its painful expressions.

As long as the human population expands, cities will expand too, regardless of whether urbanization increases or declines. This means that some individual cities will reach a size that will make 19th-century metropolises look like small towns. If the New York urbanized area should continue to grow only as fast as the nation's population (according to medium projections of the latter by the Bureau of the Census), it would reach 21 million by 1985 and 30 million by 2010. I have calculated that if India's population should grow as the UN projections indicate it will, the largest city in India in the year 2000 will have between 36 and 66 million inhabitants.

What is the implication of such giant agglomerations for

human destiny? In 1950 the New York–Northeastern New Jersey urbanized area had an average density of 9,810 persons per square mile. With 30 million people in the year 2010, the density would be 24,000 per square mile. Although this level is exceeded now in parts of New York City (which averages about 25,000 per square mile) and many other cities, it is a high density to be spread over such a big area; it would cover, remember, the suburban areas to which people moved to escape high density. Actually, however, the density of the New York urbanized region is dropping, not increasing, as the population grows. The reason is that the territory covered by the urban agglomeration is growing faster than the population: it grew by 51 percent from 1950 to 1960, whereas the population rose by 15 percent.

If, then, one projects the rise in population and the rise in territory for the New York urbanized region, one finds the density problem solved. It is not solved for long, though, because New York is not the only city in the region that is expanding. So are Philadelphia, Trenton, Hartford, New Haven and so on. By 1960 a huge stretch of territory about 600 miles long and 30 to 100 miles wide along the Eastern seaboard contained some 37 million people (I am speaking of a longer section of the seaboard than the Boston-to-Washington conurbation referred to by some other authors in this book). Since the whole area is becoming one big polynucleated city, its population cannot long expand without a rise in density. Thus persistent human multiplication promises to frustrate the ceaseless search for space— for ample residential lots, wide-open suburban school grounds, sprawling shopping centers, one-floor factories, broad freeways.

How people feel about giant agglomerations is best indicated by their headlong effort to escape them. The bigger the city, the higher the cost of space; yet, the more the level of living rises, the more people are willing to pay for low-density living. Nevertheless, as urbanized areas expand and collide, it seems probable that life in low-density surroundings will become too dear for the great majority.

One can of course imagine that cities may cease to grow and may even shrink in size while the population in general continues to multiply. Even this dream, however, would not permanently solve the problem of space. It would eventually obliterate the distinction between urban and rural, but at the expense of the rural.

It seems plain that the only way to stop urban crowding and to solve most of the urban problems besetting both the developed and the underdeveloped nations is to reduce the overall rate of population growth. Policies designed to do this have as yet little intelligence and power behind them. Urban planners continue to treat population growth as something to be planned for, not something to be itself planned. Any talk about applying brakes to city growth is therefore purely speculative, overshadowed as it is by the reality of uncontrolled population increase.

The Origin and Evolution of Cities

· GIDEON SJOBERG

The first cities arose some 5,500 years ago; large-scale urbanization began only about 100 years ago. The intervening steps in the evolution of cities were nonetheless a prerequisite for modern urban societies.

MEN BEGAN to live in cities some 5,500 years ago. As the preceding chapter relates, however, the proportion of the human population concentrated in cities did not begin to increase significantly until about 100 years ago. These facts raise two questions that this chapter proposes to answer. First, what factors brought about the origin of cities? Second, through what evolutionary stages did cities pass before the modern epoch of urbanization? The answers to these questions are intimately related to three major levels of human organization, each of which is characterized by its own technological, economic, social and political patterns. The least complex of the three—the "folk society"—is preurban and even preliterate; it consists typically of small numbers of people, gathered in self-sufficient homogeneous groups, with their energies wholly (or almost wholly) absorbed by the quest for food. Under such conditions there is little or no surplus of food; consequently the folk society permits little or no specialization of labor or distinction of class.

Although some folk societies still exist today, similar human groups began the slow process of evolving into more complex societies millenniums ago, through settlement in villages and through advances in technology and organizational structure. This gave rise to the second level of organization: civilized preindustrial, or "feudal," society. Here there is a surplus of food because of the selective cultivation of grains—high in yield, rich in biological energy and suited to long-term storage—and often also because of the practice of animal husbandry. The food surplus permits both the specialization of labor and the kind of class structure that can, for instance, provide the leadership and command the manpower to develop and maintain extensive irrigation systems (which in turn make possible further increases in the food supply). Most preindustrial societies possess metallurgy, the plow and the wheel—devices, or the means of creating devices, that multiply both the production and the distribution of agricultural surpluses.

Two other elements of prime importance characterize the civilized preindustrial stage of organization. One is writing: not only the simple keeping of accounts but also the recording of historical events, law, literature and religious beliefs. Literacy, however, is usually confined to a leisured elite. The other element is that this stage of organization has only a few sources of energy other than the muscles of men and livestock; the later preindustrial societies harnessed the force of the wind to sail the seas and grind grain and also made use of water power.

It was in the context of this second type of society that the world's first cities developed. Although preindustrial cities still survive, the modern industrial city is associated with a third level of complexity in human organization, a level characterized by mass literacy, a fluid class system and, most important, the tremendous technological breakthrough to new sources of inanimate energy that produced and still sustains the industrial revolution. Viewed against the background of this three-tiered structure, the first emergence of cities at the level of civilized preindustrial society can be more easily understood.

Two factors in addition to technological advance beyond the folk-society level were needed for cities to emerge. One was a special type of social organization by means of which the agricultural surplus produced by technological advance could be collected, stored and distributed. The same apparatus could also organize the labor force needed for large-scale construction, such as public buildings, city walls and irrigation systems. A social organization of this kind requires a variety of full-time specialists directed by a ruling elite. The latter, although few in number, must command sufficient political power—reinforced by an ideology, usually religious in character—to ensure that the peasantry periodically relinquishes a substantial part of the agricultural yield in order to support the city dwellers. The second factor required was a favorable environment, providing not only fertile soil for the peasants but also a water supply adequate for both agriculture and urban consumption. Such conditions exist in geologically mature and mid-latitude river valleys, and it was in such broad alluvial regions that the world's earliest cities arose.

What is a city? It is a community of substantial size and population density that shelters a variety of nonagricultural specialists, including a literate elite. I emphasize the role of literacy as an ingredient of urban life for good reasons. Even though writing systems took centuries to evolve, their presence or absence serves as a convenient means for distinguishing between genuinely urban communities and others that in spite of their large size and dense population must be considered quasi-urban or nonurban. This is because once a community achieves or otherwise acquires the technological advance we call writing, a major transformation in the social order occurs; with a written tradition rather than an oral one it is possible to create more complex administrative and legal systems and more rigorous systems of thought. Writing is indispensable to the development of mathematics, astronomy and the other sciences: its existence thus implies the emergence of a number of significant specializations within the social order.

As far as is known, the world's first cities took shape around 3500 B.C. in the Fertile Crescent, the eastern segment of which includes Mesopotamia: the valleys of the Tigris and the Euphrates. Not only were the soil and water supply there suitable; the region was a crossroads that facilitated repeated contacts among peoples of divergent cultures for thousands of years. The resulting mixture of alien and indigenous crafts and skills must have made its own contribution to the evolution of the first true cities out of the village settlements in lower Mesopotamia. These were primarily in Sumer but also to some extent in Akkad, a little to the north. Some—such as Eridu, Erech, Lagash and Kish—are more familiar to archaeologists than to others; Ur, a later city, is more widely known.

These early cities were much alike; for one thing, they had a similar technological base. Wheat and barley were the cereal crops, bronze was the metal, oxen pulled plows and there were wheeled vehicles. Moreover, the city's leader was both king and high priest; the peasants' tribute to the city god was stored in the temple granaries. Luxury goods recovered from royal tombs and temples attest the existence of skilled artisans, and the importation of precious metals and gems from well beyond the borders of Mesopotamia bespeaks a class of merchant-traders. Population sizes can only be guessed in the face of such unknowns as the average number of residents per household and the extent of each city's zone of influence. The excavator of Ur, Sir Leonard Woolley, estimates that soon after 2000 B.C. the city proper housed 34,000 people; in my opinion, however, it seems unlikely that, at least in the earlier periods, even the larger of these cities contained more than 5,000 to 10,000 people, including part-time farmers on the cities' outskirts.

The valley of the Nile, not too far from Mesopotamia, was also a region of early urbanization. To judge from Egyptian writings of a later time, there may have been urban communities in the Nile delta by 3100 B.C. Whether the Egyptian concept of city living had "diffused" from Mesopotamia or was independently invented (and perhaps even earlier than in Mesopotamia) is a matter of scholarly debate; in any case the initial stages of Egyptian urban life may yet be discovered deep in the silt of the delta, where scientific excavation is only now being undertaken.

Urban communities—diffused or independently invented—spread widely during the third and second millenniums B.C. By about 2500 B.C. the cities of Mohenjo-Daro and Harappa were flourishing in the valley of the Indus River in what is now Pakistan. Within another 1,000 years at the most the middle reaches of the Yellow River in China supported urban settlements. A capital city of the Shang Dynasty (about 1500 B.C.) was uncovered near An-

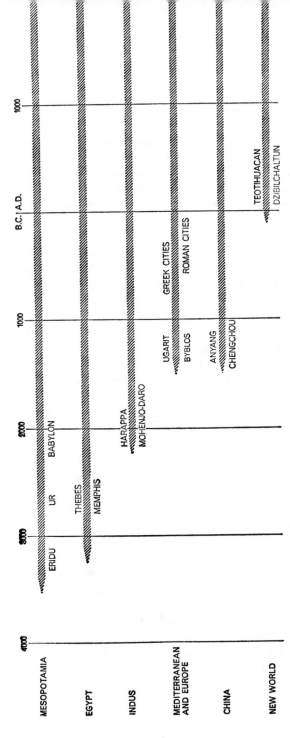

SEQUENCE of urban evolution begins with the first cities of Mesopotamia, makes its next appearance in the Nile Valley, then extends to the Indus, to the eastern Mediterranean region and at last to China. In each area, the independently urbanized New World included, cities rose and fell but urban life, once established, never wholly disappeared.

yang before World War II; current archaeological investigations
by the Chinese may well prove that city life was actually established in ancient China several centuries earlier.

The probability that the first cities of Egypt were later than
those of Sumer and the certainty that those of the Indus and
Yellow rivers are later lends weight to the argument that the concept of urban living diffused to these areas from Mesopotamia.
Be this as it may, none will deny that in each case the indigenous
population contributed uniquely to the development of the cities
in its own area.

In contrast to the situation in the Old World, it appears certain
that diffusion played an insignificant role or none at all in the
creation of the pre-Columbian cities of the New World. The
peoples of Mesoamerica—notably the Maya, the Zapotecs, the
Mixtecs and the Aztecs—evidently developed urban communities
on a major scale, the exact extent of which is only now being revealed by current investigations. Until quite recently, for example, many New World archaeologists doubted that the Maya
had ever possessed cities; it was the fashion to characterize their
impressive ruins as ceremonial centers visited periodically by the
members of a scattered rural population. It is now clear, however,
that many such centers were genuine cities. At the Maya site of
Tikal in Guatemala some 3,000 structures have been located in an
area of 6.2 square miles; only 10 percent of them are major ceremonial buildings. Extrapolating on the basis of test excavations
of more than 100 of these lesser structures, about two-thirds of
them appear to have been dwellings. If only half the present-day
average household figure for the region (5.6 members) is applied
to Tikal, its population would have been more than 5,000. At another major Maya site—Dzibilchaltun in Yucatán—a survey of less
than half of the total area has revealed more than 8,500 structures.
Teotihuacán, the largest urban site in the region of modern Mexico
City, may have had a population of 100,000 during the first millennium A.D.

Although only a few examples of writing have been identified
at Teotihuacán, it is reasonable to assume that writing was known;
there were literate peoples elsewhere in Mesoamerica at the time.
By the same token, the achievements of the Maya in such realms
as mathematics and astronomy would have forced the conclusion

that they were an urban people even in the absence of supporting archaeological evidence. Their invention of the concept of zero (evidently earlier than the Hindus' parallel feat) and their remarkably precise calculation of the length of the solar year would surely have been impossible if their literate elite had been scattered about the countryside in villages rather than concentrated in urban centers where a cross-fertilization of ideas could take place.

Mesoamerica was by no means the only area of large, dense communities in the New World; they also existed in the Andean region. A culture such as the Inca, however, cannot be classified as truly urban. In spite of—perhaps because of—their possession of a mnemonic means of keeping inventories (an assemblage of knotted cords called a quipu) the Incas lacked any conventionalized set of graphic symbols for representing speech or any concepts other than numbers and certain broad classes of items. As a result they were denied such key structural elements of an urban community as a literate elite and a written heritage of law, religion and history. Although the Incas could claim major military, architectural and engineering triumphs and apparently were on the verge of achieving a civilized order, they were still quasi-urban at the time of the European conquest, much like the Dahomey, Ashanti and Yoruba peoples of Africa.

The New World teaches us two lessons. In Mesoamerica cities were created without animal husbandry, the wheel and an extensive alluvial setting. One reason for this is maize, a superior grain crop that produced a substantial food surplus with relatively little effort and thus compensated for the limited tools and nonriverine environment. In the Andean region imposing feats of engineering and an extensive division of labor were not enough, in the absence of writing, to give rise to a truly urban society.

In spite of considerable cultural diversity among the inhabitants of the Near East, the Orient and the New World, the early cities in all these regions had a number of organizational forms in common. The dominant pattern was theocracy—the king and the high priest were one. The elite had their chief residences in the city; moreover, they and their retainers and servants congregated mainly in the city's center. This center was the prestige area, where the most imposing religious and government buildings were located

Such a concentration had dual value: in an era when communications and transport were rudimentary, propinquity enhanced interaction among the elite; at the same time it gave the ruling class maximum protection from external attack.

At a greater distance from this urban nucleus were the shops and dwellings of artisans—masons, carpenters, smiths, jewelers, potters—many of whom served the elite. The division of labor into crafts, apparent in the earliest cities, became more complex with the passage of time. Artisan groups, some of which even in early times may have belonged to specific ethnic minorities, tended to establish themselves in special quarters or streets. Such has been characteristic of preindustrial cities in all cultural settings, from the earliest times to the present day. The poorest urbanites lived on the outskirts of the city, as did part-time or full-time farmers; their scattered dwellings finally blended into open countryside.

From its inception the city, as a residence of specialists, has been a continuing source of innovation. Indeed, the very emergence of cities greatly accelerated social and cultural change; to borrow a term from the late British archaeologist V. Gordon Childe, we can properly regard the "urban revolution" as being equal in significance to the agricultural revolution that preceded it and the industrial revolution that followed it. The city acted as a promoter of change in several ways. Many of the early cities arose on major transportation routes; new ideas and inventions flowed into them quite naturally. The mere fact that a large number of specialists were concentrated in a small area encouraged innovation, not only in technology but also in religious, philosophical and scientific thought. At the same time cities could be strong bulwarks of tradition. Some—for example Jerusalem and Benares—have become sacred in the eyes of the populace; in spite of repeated destruction Jerusalem has retained this status for more than two millenniums.

The course of urban evolution can be correctly interpreted only in relation to the parallel evolution of technology and social organization (especially political organization); these are not just prerequisites to urban life but the basis for its development. As centers of innovation cities provided a fertile setting for continued technological advances; these gains made possible the further expansion of cities. Advanced technology in turn depended on the increasingly complex division of labor, particularly in the political sphere. As an example, the early urban communities of Sumer were mere city-states with restricted hinterlands, but eventually trade and commerce extended over a much broader area, enabling these cities to draw on the human and material resources of a far wider and more diverse region and even bringing about the birth of new cities. The early empires of the Iron Age—for instance the Achaemenid Empire of Persia, established early in the sixth century B.C., and the Han Empire of China, established in the third century B.C.—far surpassed in scope any of the Bronze Age. And as empires became larger the size and grandeur of their cities increased. In fact, as Childe has observed, urbanization spread more rapidly during the first five centuries of the Iron Age than it had in all 15 centuries of the Bronze Age.

In the sixth and fifth centuries B.C. the Persians expanded their empire into western Turkestan and created a number of cities, often by building on existing villages. In this expansion Toprak-kala, Merv and Marakanda (part of which was later the site of Samarkand) moved toward urban status. So too in India, at the close of the fourth century B.C., the Mauryas in the north spread their empire to the previously nonurban south and into Ceylon, giving impetus to the birth of cities such as Ajanta and Kanchi. Under the Ch'in and Han dynasties, between the third century B.C. and the third century A.D., city life took hold in most of what was then China and beyond, particularly to the south and west. The "Great Silk Road" extending from China to Turkestan became studded with such oasis cities as Suchow, Khotan and Kashgar; Nanking and Canton seem to have attained urban status at this time, as did the settlement that was eventually to become Peking.

At the other end of the Eurasian land mass the Phoenicians began toward the end of the second millennium B.C. to spread westward and to revive or establish urban life along the northern coast of Africa and in Spain. These coastal traders had by then developed a considerable knowledge of shipbuilding; this, combined with their far-reaching commercial ties and power of arms, made the Phoenicians lords of the Mediterranean for a time. Some centuries later the Greeks followed a rather similar course. Their city-states—actually in a sense small empires—created or rebuilt numerous urban outposts along the Mediterranean shore from

Asia Minor to Spain and France, and eastward to the most distant
coast of the Black Sea. The empire that did the most to diffuse city
life into the previously nonurban regions of the West—France,
Britain, the Low Countries, Germany west of the Rhine, central
and even eastern Europe—was of course Rome.

Empires are effective disseminators of urban forms because they
have to build cities with which to maintain military supremacy in
conquered regions. The city strongholds, in turn, require an administrative apparatus in order to tap the resources of the conquered area and encourage the commerce needed both to support
the military garrison and to enhance the wealth of the homeland.
Even when a new city began as a purely commercial outpost, as
was the case under the Phoenicians, some military and administrative support was necessary if it was to survive and function
effectively in alien territory.

There is a significant relation between the rise and fall of empires and the rise and fall of cities; in a real sense history is the
study of urban graveyards. The capitals of many former empires
are today little more than ghostly outlines that only hint at a
glorious past. Such was the fate of Babylon and Nineveh, Susa in
Persia, Seleucia in Mesopotamia and Vijayanagar in India. Yet
there are exceptions. Some cities have managed to survive over
long periods of time by attaching themselves first to one empire
and then to another. Athens, for example, did not decline after
the collapse of Greek power; it was able to attach itself to the
Roman Empire, which subsidized Athens as a center of learning.
Once Rome fell, however, both the population and the prestige of
Athens dwindled steadily; it was little more than a town until the
rise of modern Greece in the 19th century. On the other hand,
nearby Byzantium, a city-state of minor importance under Roman
rule, not only became the capital of the Eastern Roman Empire
and its successor, the Ottoman Empire, but as Istanbul remains a
major city to this day.

In the light of the recurrent rise and decline of cities in so many
areas of the world, one may ask just how urban life has been able
to persist and why the skills of technology and social organization
required for city-building were not lost. The answer is that the
knowledge was maintained within the framework of empires—by
means of written records and oral transmission by various special-

ists. Moreover, all empires have added to their store of skills relating to urban development as a result of diffusion—including the migration of specialists—from other civilized areas. At the same time various civilized or uncivilized subjects within empires have either been purposely educated by their conquerors or have otherwise gained access to the body of urban lore. The result on occasion is that the subjects challenge the power of the dominant ruling group.

The rise and fall of the Roman Empire provides a highly instructive case study that illuminates several relations between the life-span of cities and the formation and decline of empires. The Romans themselves took many elements of their civilization from the Etruscans, the Greeks and other civilized peoples who came under their sway. After Rome's northward expansion in western Europe and the proliferation of Roman cities in regions inhabited by so-called "barbarians"—in this instance preliterate, or "noncivilized," peoples—the Roman leaders were simply unable to staff all the bureaucratic posts with their own citizens. Some of the preliterates had to be trained to occupy such posts both in their own homelands and in the cities on the frontier. This process made it possible for the Romans to exploit the wealth of conquered regions and may have pacified the subjugated groups for a time, but in the long run it engendered serious conflicts. Eventually the Ostrogoths, Vandals, Burgundians and others—having been partially urbanized, having developed a literate elite of their own and having acquired many Roman technological and administrative skills—turned against the imperial power structure and engineered the collapse of Rome and its empire. Nor is this a unique case in history; analogics can be perceived in the modern independence movements of such European colonies as those in Africa.

With the breakup of the Roman Empire, not only did the city of Rome (which at its largest may have had more than 300,000 inhabitants) decline markedly but many borderland cities disappeared or shrank to small towns or villages. The decline was dramatic, but it is too often assumed that after the fall of Rome cities totally disappeared from western Europe. The historian E. Ewig has recently shown that many cities continued to function, particularly in Italy and southern France. Here, as in all civilized societies, the surviving cities were the chief residences and centers of activity for the political and religious elite who commanded the positions of power and privilege that persisted during the so-called Dark Ages.

In spite of Rome's decline many of the techniques and concepts associated with literate traditions in such fields as medicine and astronomy were kept alive; this was done both in the smaller surviving urban communities of Europe and in the eastern regions that had been ruled by the Romans—notably in the cities of the succeeding Eastern Roman Empire. Some of the technology and learning associated with Rome also became the basis for city life in the Arab empires that arose later in the Near East, North Africa, Spain and even central Asia. Indeed, the Byzantine and Arab empires—which had such major intellectual centers as Constantinople, Antioch, Damascus, Cairo and Baghdad—advanced beyond the knowledge inherited from antiquity. The Arabs, for example, took from the Hindus the concept of zero and the decimal system of numerals; by utilizing these concepts in both theory and practice they achieved significant advances over the knowledge that had evolved in the West. Eventually much of the new learning was passed on to Europe, where it helped to build the foundations for the industrial revolution.

In time Europe reestablished extensive commercial contact with the Byzantine and Arab empires; the interchange that followed played a significant role in the resurgence of urban life in southern Europe. The revitalization of trade was closely associated with the formation of several prosperous Italian city-states in the 10th and 11th centuries A.D. Venice and other cities eventually were transformed into small-scale empires whose colonies were scattered over the Mediterranean region—a hinterland from which the home cities were able to extract not only many of their necessities but also luxury items. By A.D. 1000 Venice had forged commercial links with Constantinople and other cities of the Eastern Roman Empire, partly as a result of the activities of the Greek colony in Venice. The Venetians were able to draw both on the knowledge of these resident Greeks and on the practical experience of sea captains and other specialists among them. Such examples make it clear that the Italian city-states were not merely local creations but rather products of a multiplicity of cultural forces.

Beginning at the turn of the 11th century A.D. many European cities managed to win a kind of independence from the rulers of the various principalities and petty kingdoms that surrounded them. Particularly in northern Italy urban communities came to enjoy considerable political autonomy. This provided an even more favorable atmosphere for commerce and encouraged the growth of such urban institutions as craft guilds. The European pattern is quite different from that in most of Asia (for instance in India and China), where the city was never able to attain a measure of autonomy within the broader political structure. At the same time the extent of self-rule enjoyed by the medieval European cities can be exaggerated and often is; by the close of the Middle Ages urban self-rule was already beginning to be lost. It is therefore evident that the political autonomy of medieval cities was only indirectly related to the eventual evolution of the industrial city.

It was the industrial revolution that brought about truly far-reaching changes in city life. In some nations today, as Kingsley Davis notes in the preceding chapter, the vast majority of the inhabitants are city dwellers; nearly 80 percent of the people in the United Kingdom live in cities, as do nearly 70 percent of the people of the U.S. Contrast this with the preindustrial civilized world, in which only a small, socially dominant minority lived in cities. The industrial revolution has also led to fundamental changes in the city's social geography and social organization; the industrial city is marked by a greater fluidity in the class system, the appearance of mass education and mass communications and the shift of some of the elite from the center of the city to its suburban outskirts.

Although there are still insufficient data on the rise of the industrial city—an event that took place sometime between 1750 and 1850—and although scholars disagree over certain steps in the process, the major forces at work in the two or three centuries before the industrial city emerged can be perceived clearly enough. Viewed in the light of Europe's preindustrial urban era, two factors are evident: the expansion of European power into other continents and the development of a technology based on inanimate rather than animate sources of energy. The extension of European trade and exploration (which was to culminate in European colonialism) not only induced the growth of cities in Asia, in parts of nonurban Africa and in the Americas but also helped to raise the standard of living of Europeans themselves and made possible the support of more specialists. Notable among the last was a new occupational group—the scientists. The expansion abroad had helped to shatter the former world view of European scholars; they were now forced to cope with divergent ideas and customs. The discoveries reported by the far-ranging European explorers thus gave added impetus to the advance of science.

The knowledge gained through the application of the scientific method is the one factor above all others that made the modern city possible. This active experimental approach has enabled man to control the forces of nature to an extent undreamed of in the preindustrial era. It is true that in the course of several millenniums the literate elite of the preindustrial cities added significantly to man's store of knowledge in such fields as medicine, astronomy and mathematics, but these scholars generally scorned mundane activities and avoided contact with those whose work was on the practical level. This meant that the scholars' theories were rarely tested and applied in the everyday realm. Moreover, in accordance with prevailing religious thought, man was not to tamper with the natural order or to seek to control it, in either its physical or its social aspect. For example, medical scholars in Greek and Roman cities did not dissect human cadavers; not until the 16th century in Europe did a physician—Andreas Vesalius of Brussels—actually use findings obtained from dissection to revise ancient medical theories.

In the field of engineering, as late as the 17th century most advances were made by artisans who worked more or less on a trial-and-error basis. With the development of the experimental method, however, the learning of the elite became linked with the practical knowledge of the artisan, the barber-surgeon and the like; the result was a dramatic upsurge of knowledge and a fundamental revision of method that has been termed the scientific revolution. Such was the basis of the industrial revolution and the industrial city.

That the first industrial cities appeared in England is hardly fortuitous; England's social structure lacked the rigidity that characterized most of Europe and the rest of the civilized world. The Puritan tradition in England—an ethical system that supports utilitarianism and empiricism—did much to alter earlier views concerning man's place in nature. In England scholars could communicate with artisans more readily than elsewhere in Europe.

The advent of industrialism brought vast improvements in agricultural implements, farming techniques and food preservation, as well as in transportation and communication. Improved water supplies and more effective methods of sewage disposal allowed more people to congregate in cities. Perhaps the key invention was the steam engine, which provided a new and much more bountiful source of energy. Before that time, except for power from wind and water, man had no energy resources other than human and animal muscle. Now the factory system, with its mass production of goods and mechanization of activity, began to take hold. With it emerged a new kind of occupational structure: a structure that depends on highly specialized knowledge and that functions effectively only when the activities of the component occupations are synchronized. This process of industrialization has not only continued unabated to the present day but has actually accelerated with the rise of self-controlling machines.

The evolution of the industrial city was not an unmixed blessing. Historians have argued through many volumes the question of whether the new working class, including many migrants from the countryside, lost or gained economically and socially as the factory system destroyed older social patterns. Today, as industrialization moves inexorably across the globe, it continues to create social problems. Many surviving traditional cities evince in various ways the conflict between their preindustrial past and their industrial future. Nonetheless, the trend is clear: barring nuclear war, the industrial city will become the dominant urban form throughout the world, replacing forever the preindustrial city that was man's first urban creation.

The Modern Metropolis

· HANS BLUMENFELD

The urban revolution that began in the latter half of the 19th century has culminated in a qualitatively new kind of human settlement: an extended urban area with a dense central city.

THE PRECEDING CHAPTER is entitled "The Origin and Evolution of Cities"; in this chapter we speak of the product of that evolution not as "the modern city" but as "the modern metropolis." The change of name reflects the fact that from its long, slow evolution the city has emerged into a revolutionary stage. It has undergone a qualitative change, so that it is no longer merely a larger version of the traditional city but a new and different form of human settlement.

There is some argument about the term. Lewis Mumford objects to "metropolis" (from the Greek words for "mother" and "city"), which historically had a very different meaning; he prefers the term "conurbation," coined by Patrick Geddes, the Scottish biologist who was a pioneer in city planning. This word, however, implies formation by the fusion of several preexisting cities; most metropolises did not originate in that way. The term "megalopolis," coined by the French geographer Jean Gottmann, is generally applied to an urbanized region that contains several metropolitan areas, such as the region extending from Boston to Washington. On the whole it seems best to retain the term "metropolis," now commonly adopted in many languages as the name for a major city center and its environs.

"Metropolitan area" can be defined in various ways; the U.S. Bureau of the Census, for instance, defines it as any area containing a nuclear city of at least 50,000 population. The new phenomenon we are considering, however, is a much bigger entity with a certain minimum critical size. In agreement with the German scholar Gerhard Isenberg, I shall define a metropolis as a concentration of at least 500,000 people living within an area in which the traveling time from the outskirts to the center is no more than about 40 minutes. Isenberg and I have both derived this definition from observations of the transformation of cities into metropolises during the first half of the 20th century. At the present time—at least in North America—the critical mass that distinguishes a metropolis from the traditional city can be considerably larger—perhaps nearing one million population.

The emergence of a basically new form of human settlement is an extremely rare event in the history of mankind. For at least 5,000 years all civilizations have been characterized predominantly by just two well-marked types of settlement: the farm village and the city. Until recently the vast majority of the population lived in villages. They produced not only their own raw materials—food, fuel and fiber—but also the manufactured goods and services they required. The cities were inhabited by only a small minority of the total population, generally less than 20 percent. These people were the ruling elite—the religious, political, military and commercial leaders—and the retinue of laborers, craftsmen and professionals who served them. The elite drew their subsistence and power from the work of the villagers by collecting tithes, taxes or rent. This system prevailed until the end of the 18th century, and its philosophy was well expressed by physiocrats of that time on both sides of the Atlantic, including Thomas Jefferson.

The industrial revolution dramatically reversed the distribution of population between village and city. A German contemporary of Jefferson's, Justus Moeser, foresaw at the very beginning of the revolution what was to come; he observed that "specialized division of labor forces workers to live in big cities." With increasing specialization there had to be increased cooperation of labor, both within and between establishments. The division of labor and increased productivity made concentration in cities possible, and the required cooperation of labor made it necessary, because the new system called for bringing together workers of many skills and diverse establishments that had to interchange goods and services.

The process fed on itself, growth inducing further growth. Many economists have noted that the rapid rise of productivity has been largely instrumental in bringing about a progressive shift of the main part of the labor force from the primary industry of raw-material production to the secondary industry of material processing and finally to the tertiary industry of services. Less attention has been paid to a related, equally important factor behind this shift, namely the "specializing out" of functions. The farmer's original functions of producing his own motive power (work animals), fuel (hay and oats), tools, building materials and consumer goods have been specialized out to secondary industries that supply him with tractors, gasoline and his other necessities. Today, in the tertiary stage, much of the work connected with secondary industry is being specialized out to purveyors of business services (accounting, control, selling, distribution). Even the functions of the household itself (personal services, housekeeping, repairs, shopping, recreation, education) are taken over by consumer-service industries.

The dual spur of specialization and cooperation of labor started a great wave of migration from country to city all over the globe. In the advanced countries the 19th-century development of long-distance transportation by steamship and railroad and of communication by the electric telegraph made it possible for cities to draw on large regions and grow to populations of millions. For a time their growth was limited by internal restrictions. Travel within the city still had to be by foot or by hoof. A New York businessman could communicate quickly with his partners in Shanghai by cablegram, but to deliver an order to an office a few blocks away he had to send a messenger. This situation limited cities to a radius of only about three miles from the center. In the absence of elevators the city was also limited in vertical expansion. The only possible growth was interstitial, by covering every square inch of available space. Residences, factories, shops and offices all crowded close together around the center. The result was a fantastic rise in the price of city land compared with the cost of the structures that could be built on it.

This was only a transitory phase in the growth of the city, but its heritage is still with us, in structures, street patterns, institutions and concepts. We still think and talk and act in terms of "city and country" and "city and suburb," although these concepts have lost meaning in the modern metropolis and its region. The transformation was set in motion toward the end of the 19th century and early in the 20th with the invention of the telephone, the electric streetcar, the subway and the powered elevator. Even more far-reaching was the impact on the city of the automobile and the truck. With the acquisition of these aids to communication and mobility the city burst its eggshell and emerged as a metropolis. (It is worth noting that the telephone and the automobile had equally profound effects on rural life, fragmenting the old farm village and giving rise to huge, scattered farms.)

The centripetal migration from the country to the city continues unabated, but now there is an equally powerful centrifugal wave of migration from the city to the suburbs. Although on a national scale more and more of the population is becoming urban, within the urban areas there is increasing decentralization. The interaction of these two trends has produced the new form of settlement we call the metropolis. It is no longer a "city" as that institution has been understood in the past, but on the other hand it is certainly not "country" either. The fact that it is neither one nor the other has aroused nostalgic critics, who appeal for a return to "true urbanity" and to a "real countryside." But in view of the inexorable technological and economic trends that have created the metropolis these terms also require a new and different interpretation.

It has become fashionable to describe the transformation of the city into the metropolis as an "explosion." The term is misleading on two counts. The change is not destroying the city, as "explosion" implies, nor is it a sudden, unheralded event. The movement of population from the center of the city outward to an ever expanding periphery has been going on for at least a century. In the metropolitan region of New York, New Jersey and Connecticut, where the average density of population within the cities and towns of the area increased steadily up to 1860, it began to drop after that date. The outward spread of the city was nearly as strong between 1860 and 1900 as it has been since 1900. In Philadelphia the population movement away from the center of the city was actually proportionately greater in the half century between 1860 and 1910 than in the period 1900 to 1950.

Analysis of the population density in the metropolitan area of Philadelphia and that of other cities shows that the centrifugal wave of movement to the suburbs has proceeded with amazing regularity. From the center of the city out to the periphery at any one time there is a consistent decline in residential density from one zone to the next. As time has passed, the curve representing this decline has become less steep; that is, the center has lost or stood still in density while the outer areas have gained, so that the difference between them is less. Interestingly, the density gradient from the center to the periphery has also become smoother (that is, less lumped around outer towns), which seems to indicate that the center is actually strengthening its influence over the outer areas. In each zone the rise in density with time eventually flattens out, as if the density has reached a "saturation" level for that zone; this level is lower for each successive zone out to the periphery. With the passage of time the crest of the wave (the zone of fastest growth) moves outward in a regular fashion. The innermost zone at the center of the city seems to show an anomaly, in that its population density is lower than that of the surrounding area, but this merely reflects the fact that the center is occupied predominantly by stores and offices. If its daytime working population were included in the census, it would have a far higher density.

One can outline a "natural history" of the modern metropolis. The metropolis is characterized first of all by a certain measure of mutual accessibility among its various parts, which determines its total size. As I have mentioned, in most cases the area embraced by the metropolis has a radius represented by a traveling time of about 40 minutes in the principal vehicle of transportation (train or auto), or about 45 minutes from door to door. With improvement in the speed of transportation the extent of the metropolis in miles can, of course, expand. In most metropolitan areas the average travel time to work for the working population as a whole is about half an hour. No more than 15 percent of the workers spend more than 45 minutes in the daily journey to work.

This may sound surprising in view of the frequent complaints of commuters about the length of their journey. The complaints are not new. A century ago a German observer declared that the distance people on the outskirts of cities had to travel to work had reached the limit of what was bearable. Probably the range of travel times to work then was wider than it is in the metropolis today. There are strong indications, however, that the half-hour average has been more or less standard. In most American small towns, although a majority of the workers are employed within the town, a sizable minority do travel long distances to work in other communities, usually because they cannot find a job in the hometown and must seek work elsewhere but do not wish to change their home.

It is one of the great advantages of the metropolis that people can change jobs without moving their homes. Breadth of choice—for workers, for employers and for consumers—is the essence of the metropolis. The worker has a choice of employers; the employer can find workers of a wide variety of skills, including professional and managerial. Even more important is the accessibility of a variety of goods and services on which any business enterprise depends. Only a metropolis can support the large inventories, transportation facilities and specialized services—particularly those of a financial, legal, technical and promotional nature —that are essential to modern business. Such services constitute the main source of economic strength of the metropolis—its true economic base. They are especially important to small, new and experimental enterprises. The metropolis, in particular its central area, therefore serves as an incubator for such enterprises. Contrary to a common impression, the big city is most suitably a home for small industries rather than large industrial complexes. The big plant, being more nearly self-sufficient, may often be as well off in a small town. This fact is reflected in the statistics of employment: in most metropolises the number of people that are employed in manufacturing is decreasing, relatively and sometimes absolutely, while the number that are employed in services is increasing rapidly.

What is true of business services is also true of consumer services: the metropolis attracts the consumer because it offers a wide freedom of choice. Only the large population of a metropolis can support the great proliferation of special services found in the big city: large department stores, many specialty shops, opera houses, art galleries, theaters, sports stadia, special schools, large and well-equipped institutions for medical care and adult education and a host of other necessities for the full life.

To sum up, the modern metropolis differs from the traditional city in several crucial respects: (1) it combines the function of central leadership with the functions of providing the main bulk of material production and services; (2) its population is up to 10 times larger than that of the biggest preindustrial city; (3) with modern fast transportation, which has increased its commuting radius about tenfold, it is up to 100 times larger in area than the biggest city of former times; (4) it is neither city nor country but a complex of urban districts and open areas; (5) its residential and work areas are no longer combined in one place but are located in separate districts; (6) its workers have high mobility in the choice of jobs and occupations.

The feedback cycle of metropolitan growth enlarging freedom of choice and freedom of choice in turn attracting further growth has given the metropolis amazing vitality and staying power. In the premetropolis era cities laid low by war, pestilence or loss of prestige were often abandoned or reduced to weak shadows of their former glory. Even Rome became little more than a village after it lost its empire. In contrast, all the big cities destroyed in World War II have been rebuilt, most of them to beyond their prewar size. Particularly significant is the experience of Leningrad. During the Russian Revolution and again in World War II it lost about half of its population. Moreover, the revolution ended its former role as the center of government and finance and deprived it of most of its markets and sources of supply. Yet the population of Leningrad is now four million—four times what it was in 1921. This growth is especially remarkable in view of the Soviet government's policy of restricting the growth of the major cities, a policy based on Karl Marx's condemnation of big cities because of their pollution of air, water and soil. As a metropolis Leningrad is an outstanding testament to the viability of the species.

Attempts to halt the growth of the big city have been made ever since the phenomenon first appeared on the human scene. They have been singularly unsuccessful. Elizabeth I of England and after her Oliver Cromwell tried to limit the growth of London by circling it with an enforced greenbelt, but this method failed. In any case such a device, applied to a growing city, can only lead to overcrowding. To avoid big-city problems nearly all countries today have embarked on programs of industrial decentralization, often with unsatisfactory results. In the Western nations the most far-reaching attempt at decentralization is Great Britain's "new towns" plan. This program has been eminently successful in creating new centers of industry as "growth points," but it has not availed to stop the growth of London or to limit other cities, new or old, to their planned size. Significantly, all but one of the 17 new towns built in Britain since the war are satellite towns within previously existing metropolitan regions.

The U.S.S.R., by virtue of centralized planning and ownership, has been able to carry out decentralization on a continental scale. Its program has been remarkably effective in slowing the growth of Moscow and promoting that of smaller cities. Between 1939 and 1959 the towns in the U.S.S.R. with populations of less than 200,000 grew by 84 percent; those in the 200,000-to-500,000 class grew 63 percent; those in the 500,000-to-one-million class grew 48 percent, and Moscow itself increased only 20 percent in population. Moscow has, however, gone well beyond the limit of five million that the government planned: it is now at six million, nearly four times the city's population in 1921.

In the U.S., where the forces of the market rather than central planning determine industrial locations, the growth rates in the decade 1950–1960 were 27 percent in metropolitan areas of 50,000 to 500,000 population and 35 percent in those of 500,000 to two million population. In the metropolises with a population of more than two million the average growth rate was smaller: 23 percent. This average, however, was heavily weighted by the comparatively slow-growing centers of the Northeastern sector of the nation; in Los Angeles and San Francisco, the only two metropolises of this class outside the Northeast, the growth was far above the national average for all metropolitan areas.

There is no denying that the growth of the huge metropolises has brought serious problems, chief among which are traffic congestion and the pollution of air and water by smoke, household wastes, detergents and gasoline fumes. Many cities also object that the metropolis can exist only by draining the countryside of its economic, demographic and social strength. These problems are not essentially unsolvable, however. Effective methods for control of pollution exist; they need to be applied [see "The Metabolism of Cities," by Abel Wolman, page 156]. The economic and social complaints about the metropolis seem to have little substance today. The city now repays the country in full in economic terms, as we have noted, and with the improvement in sanitation and lowering of the high 19th-century urban death rate it contributes its share of the natural population increase.

The most persistent accusation against the metropolis is that it has dissolved the family and neighborhood ties that existed in the small town and has produced anomie: the absence of any values or standards of behavior. This is questionable. A number of sociological studies in metropolises of North America and western Europe have shown that family ties remain very much alive and that a considerable amount of informal community organization can be found even in their slums.

In considering the future of the metropolis the central question is that of crowding. How much bigger can the metropolis grow? Will it eventually be "choked to death" by its own growth? Data are available for examining these questions.

It is widely believed that in a big metropolis there can only be a choice between crowding together at high densities or spending an excessive amount of time traveling to work. Actually a reasonable travel radius from a central point takes in an amazing amount of territory. At an overall travel rate of 20 miles per hour, typical for present rush-hour trips from the center to the periphery in the largest American metropolitan areas, a radius of one hour's travel describes a circle with a total area of about 1,250 square miles. No more than 312 square miles would be required to house 10 million people if they lived in single-family houses on 30-by-

100-foot lots. Including streets, schools and other neighborhood facilities, the total area needed for residential use would amount to about 500 square miles. Commercial, industrial and other non-residential facilities could be accommodated amply on 150 square miles. There would be left, then, some 600 square miles, almost half of the total area within an hour's distance from the center, for parks, golf courses, forests, farms and lakes.

If the travel speed were increased to 30 miles per hour, quite feasible for both private and public transportation, the area within an hour's distance from the center could accommodate 15 million people in single-family houses on 60-by-100-foot lots, take care of all business uses and leave 1,000 square miles of open land. It may be objected that an hour is an excessive time to spend in travel to work. In practice, however, the radius from the center to the periphery would not represent the traveling distance for most workers. Relatively few would live close to the periphery, and most of these would be working at places near home rather than in the center of the city. In a metropolis of such dimensions only a small minority would have to travel more than 45 minutes to their jobs.

Evidently, then, the modern metropolis does not inherently necessitate either very high residential densities or excessively long journeys to work. The problem in planning it therefore lies in achieving a rational distribution of its components and a suitable organization of transportation facilities to connect the components.

What are the major components of the metropolis? Basically there are four: (1) the central business complex, (2) manufacturing and its allied industries, (3) housing with the attendant services and (4) open land. Let us examine each in turn.

The central area epitomizes the essence of the metropolis: mutual accessibility. It attracts particularly those functions that serve the metropolis as a whole and those that require a considerable amount of close interpersonal contact. The most conspicuous occupant of the center is diversified retail business: large department stores and specialty shops. It is surpassed in importance, however, by the closely interrelated complex of business services that occupy the giant office buildings characteristic of the central area of a metropolis: the headquarters of corporations, financial institutions and public administration and the professionals who serve them, such as lawyers, accountants and organizations engaged in promotion and public relations. Also grouped in the central area with these two categories of services are various supporting establishments, including eating and drinking places, hotels, job printers and many others.

Surprisingly, surveys show that, in spite of the recent proliferation of new office skyscrapers in the center of cities, the size of the working population in the central areas of the largest American metropolises has not actually increased over the past 30 years. Toronto, a smaller and newer metropolis, shows the same constancy in the number of central workers during the past 13 years. The explanation lies simply in the fierce competition for and the rising cost of the limited space in the center; it has caused an outward movement of those functions that can conveniently relocate farther out. Housing in the main moved out long ago; manufacturing and warehousing have tended to follow suit; so has a considerable part of the retail trade, and some of the routine business services that do not require continuous contact with their clients have also moved to less expensive locations away from the center. Modern means of communication have made this spatial separation possible. Moreover, the growth of population and purchasing power in the peripheral areas has provided bases of support there for large shopping centers, including department stores, and for many business and consumer services.

All of this indicates that the central area is undergoing a qualitative change in the direction of concentration on "higher-order" functions and at the same time is maintaining stability in quantitative terms. The forces of the market act to control overcrowding of the center. There is not much basis for the widespread fear that the metropolis will choke itself to death by uncontrolled growth.

As for manufacturing and its satellite activities, the increasing volume of production and changing technology, with a consequent requirement for more space, have made their move out to the periphery of the metropolis imperative. This is true of factories, warehouses, railroad yards, truck terminals, airports, harbor facilities and many other establishments. Three technical factors are at work: the increasing mechanization and automation of production, which calls for more floor area per worker; a switch from the traditional multistory loft building to the one-story plant, which demands more ground area; the new practice of providing open land around the plant for parking, landscaping and plant expansion. The combined effect of these three factors has been to raise the amount of land per worker in the modern factory as much as 100 times over that occupied by the old loft building.

The next major category of land use in the metropolis—housing—accounts for the largest amount of occupied land. It also presents the greatest ills of the metropolis: slums and segregation of people by income and race.

In all metropolises the low-income families tend to be segregated in the older, high-density areas toward the center of the city. This is not by choice but because they cannot afford the prices or rents of the more spacious new homes in the outer areas. The alarming result of the centrifugal movement of new residences toward the periphery is an increasing segregation of the population by income, which in the U.S. is compounded (and partly obscured) by segregation by race. The situation is more disquieting in the metropolis than it was in the smaller city or town. There, although the poor lived in older, shabbier houses, they at least shared the schools and other public facilities with the higher-income groups. In the metropolis the people living in low-income districts, particularly the housewives and children, never even meet or come to know the rest of their fellow citizens.

Poor families are effectively prevented from moving to new housing in the suburbs not only by economic inability but also by deliberate policies of the suburban governments. Squeezed between rising expenses and inadequate tax resources, these governments have quite understandably used their power of zoning and other controls to keep out housing that does not pay its way in tax revenue. More recently the central cities have adopted policies that have much the same effect. Their programs of slum clearance and redevelopment, financed in the U.S. by the National Housing Act, have failed to replace the housing they have destroyed with sufficient new housing at rents the displaced families can afford [see "The Renewal of Cities," by Nathan Glazer, page 175]. It should be obvious that housing conditions cannot be improved by decreasing the supply. Half a century ago Geddes observed: "The policy of sweeping clearance should be recognized for what I believe it is: one of the most disastrous and pernicious blunders . . . the large populations thus expelled would be . . . driven into creating worse congestion in other quarters."

Obviously the blight of slums and class segregation can be overcome only by enabling the lower-income groups to live in decent houses in desirable locations, primarily in the expanding peripheral areas, along with the middle and upper classes. The annual cost of such a program in the U.S. has been estimated at $2 billion—a modest sum compared with the amounts allotted to less constructive purposes in the national budget.

The fourth major category of metropolitan land use—open land—consists in North America at present mainly of large tracts held privately for future development. With increasing leisure there is a growing need to turn some of this land to recreational uses. In this connection we should also look at the "metropolitan region," which takes in considerably more area than the metropolis itself.

Donald J. Bogue of the University of Michigan, examining 67 metropolitan centers in the U.S., has shown that the sphere of influence of a large metropolis usually extends out to about 60 to 100 miles from the center. Typically the metropolitan region includes a number of industrial satellite towns that draw on the resources of the metropolis. The metropolis in turn looks outward to the region for various facilities, particularly recreational resorts such as large parks, lakes, summer cottages, camps, motels and lodges. In Sweden, C. F. Ahlberg, head of the Stockholm Regional Plan, has emphasized this role of the region around the capital city by naming it the "Summer Stockholm"—the widened horizon that opens up for Stockholmers when the snows have gone. Metropolises do, of course, have their winter horizons as well, typified by the ski resorts that flourish as satellites within driving distance of many an American city.

Increasingly the outer-fringe metropolitan region is becoming a popular place for retirement for people on pensions or other modest incomes who can live inexpensively in the country without being too far from the amenities of the city. This is an intriguing reversal of the ancient pattern in which the countryside was the locus of productive work and the city was the Mecca for the enjoyment of leisure.

While we are on the subject of the metropolitan region, I should like to clarify the distinction between such a region and a "conurbation" or "megalopolis." The predominant form of the metropolis is mononuclear: it derives its identity from a single center. This is the way metropolitan areas are generally organized in the U.S. and it is the only form they take in a new young settlement such as Australia, where the population is concentrated mainly in five large metropolitan areas, each centered on a single city. In the older countries of Europe, on the other hand, conurbations—metropolitan regions formed by the gradual growing together of neighboring cities—are fairly common. The outstanding examples are the cities of the Ruhr in Germany and the circle of cities that form what is known as "Randstad Holland" (including Amsterdam, Haarlem, Leiden, The Hague, Rotterdam and Utrecht). The Ruhr conurbation grew up around the coal mines. Along the French-Italian Riviera a conurbation now seems to be developing around seashore play.

There seems to be a general disposition to assume that the Boston-to-Washington axis is destined soon to become a new conurbation on a vastly larger scale than any heretofore. The available evidence does not support such a view. Each of the metropolitan areas along the seaboard remains strongly oriented to its own center. The several metropolitan regions are separated by large areas of sparse development. Conurbation can occur only when the crests of the waves of two expanding centers overlap, and except perhaps between Washington and Baltimore that is not likely to happen anywhere in North America during this century.

To get back to the problems of planning for the metropolis: How should the four main components—central business, production, residence and open land—be organized spatially? The aims here can be expressed most clearly in the form of pairs of seemingly contradictory requirements.

First, it is desirable to minimize the need for commuting to work and at the same time maximize the ability to do so. Obviously most people would like to live close to their place of work, but to seek such an arrangement as a general proposition would be unrealistic and too restrictive. It is estimated that half of all metropolitan households contain more than one gainfully employed person, and they are not likely to be employed in the same place. Furthermore, the preferred locations for residence and work do not necessarily match up. The situation in Hudson County, N.J., across the river from Manhattan, offers a striking illustration. In 1960 the county contained 244,000 jobs and 233,000 employed residents—apparently a neat balance. On analysis, however, it turns out that 35 percent of the jobs in the county were held by people who commuted from homes elsewhere, and 32 percent of the workers who lived in the county commuted out to work. Freedom of choice, both of the place to live and of the place to work, will always depend on opportunity to travel from one place to the other.

A second ideal of planning is to provide quick access to the center of the city and also quick access to the open country. Most people have tried to achieve a compromise by moving to the suburbs. The resulting pattern of urban sprawl, however, has made this move self-defeating. The more people move out to the suburbs, the farther they have to move from the city and the farther the country moves away from them.

Third, the functions of the metropolis must be integrated, yet there are also strong reasons to separate them—for example, to separate residences from factories or offices. Isolation of the functions by rigid zoning, however, threatens to break up the metropolis into barren and monotonous precincts. Evidently there is no pat answer to this problem. The optimal grain of mixture will vary with conditions.

Fourth, the social health of the metropolis requires that its people identify themselves both with their own neighborhood or group and with the metropolis as a whole. Since identification with an ingroup often leads to hostility toward outgroups, great emphasis is needed on measures that create interest and pride in the metropolis.

Fifth, the metropolis must strike a balance between continuity and receptiveness to change, between the traditions that give it identity and the flexibility necessary for growth and adaptation to new conditions.

Most of the schemes that have been proposed for shaping the future growth of the metropolis are tacitly based on these criteria,

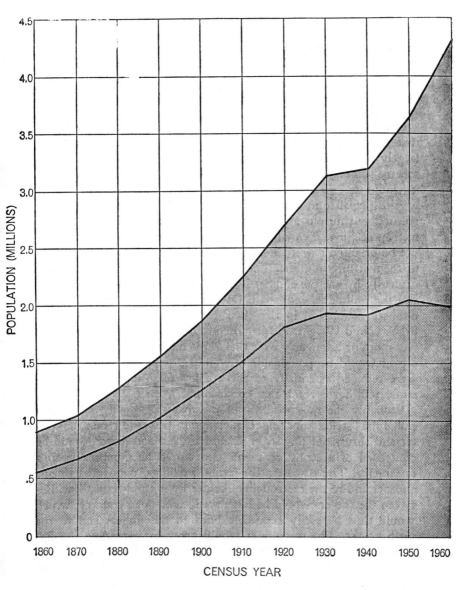

PATTERN OF METROPOLITAN GROWTH around a traditional city center is reflected in this chart giving population figures for Philadelphia (lower curve) and its outlying counties (upper curve). The entire region grew at roughly the same rate as the city until 1920. In recent years the region has burgeoned but growth of the city has declined slightly.

although the requirements have not generally been spelled out in precisely this form. The plans are designed to decentralize the metropolis in some way, with the dual aim of minimizing traffic congestion at the center and bringing the city closer to the countryside.

One proposal is the satellite plan I have already mentioned. In that arrangement each of the satellite towns outside the center is largely self-sufficient and more or less like the others. Another scheme somewhat similar to this is called the "constellation" plan; it would set up several widely separated units each of which would specialize in one function, such as finance, administration, cultural institutions and so on. Still another plan is the "linear" metropolis, several variants of which have been proposed. It would not be oriented toward a single center but would contain a series of them strung in a line. The advocates of this plan are attracted primarily by the possibilities it offers for easy access to open land and for unlimited expansion. Decentralization was pushed to its ultimate conclusion in the "Broadacre City" plan suggested by Frank Lloyd Wright. He proposed to disperse the activities of the city more or less evenly over the whole metropolitan region. Such a plan would be practicable only if the time and cost of travel were reduced essentially to zero. They may approach but certainly will never reach that condition.

Probably the most realistic of the many proposals is the plan called the "stellar" or "finger" metropolis. It would retain the center and thrust out fingers in all directions. Each finger would be composed of a string of towns and would be comparable to a linear city. The towns in the string would be connected to one another and to the metropolitan center by a rapid-transit line. Between the fingers would be large wedges of open country, which would thus be easily accessible both to the fingers and to the main center. The metropolis would grow by extending the fingers. This outline is the basis of current plans for the future development of Copenhagen and Stockholm and of the "Year 2000" plan for Washington, D.C.

Any plan that seeks to control the growth of the metropolis rather than leaving it to the play of market forces will require the setting up of new forms of control. Because it inevitably entails transfers of value from one piece of land to another, planning of any sort is bound to come into conflict with the existing vested interests of landowners and municipalities. It is obvious, therefore, that the implementation of rational regional planning would call for: (1) the creation of an overall metropolitan government for the metropolis, (2) public ownership of all or most of the land that is to be developed, (3) tax revenues sufficient to enable the metropolitan government to acquire the land and carry out the public works required for its development, (4) a national housing policy that would eliminate segregation by providing people at all income levels with freedom of choice in the location of their dwellings.

In terms of current American political folklore these are radical measures. Each of them, however, has been carried out in varying forms and to a varying degree by more than one European nation within the framework of democratic capitalism.

In the long run the development of the metropolis is likely to be influenced most powerfully by improvements in transportation and communication and by the increase in leisure time. The first may lead to an expansion of the metropolis that will embrace a whole region. The second, depending on future developments in mankind's social structure and culture, may lead to *panem et circenses* ("bread and circuses") or to *otium cum dignitate* ("leisure with dignity"). Both are possible in the metropolis.

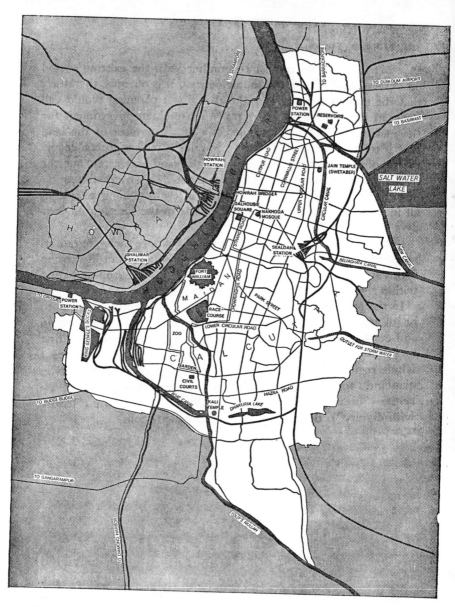

CITY OF CALCUTTA was founded by traders of the British East India Company in 1690 around a nucleus of Hooghly River villages in the Ganges delta some 70 miles inland from the Bay of Bengal. The modern Fort William (center of map) and its surrounding two square miles of maidan, or park, were carefully laid out in 1757, but the rest of the urban area along both banks of the river grew without benefit of plan. Some parts lie below high-water level; the flat terrain makes drainage in general difficult. The seat of the British government of India until 1912, Calcutta remains India's largest city today. Some three million people live within the 40 square miles outlined in the map, and nearly seven million live in the 400 square miles of the Calcutta Metropolitan District.

Calcutta: a Premature Metropolis

· NIRMAL KUMAR BOSE

The first of four chapters on cities that exemplify diverse urban situations. Calcutta has become a metropolis without benefit of the industrial revolution that gave rise to cities in advanced nations.

OF THE 250-ODD CITIES in the world that have populations of 500,-000 or more, nearly half are in the developing countries. These cities have arisen out of phase with history: they have appeared in the setting of the traditional agricultural economy in advance of the industrial revolution that is supposed to beget the metropolis [see "The Modern Metropolis," by Hans Blumenfeld, page 40]. One of these cities is Calcutta. India's largest urban center, the metropolitan district of Calcutta crowds nearly seven million people into its 400 square miles. Calcutta is not only a great seaport and today an increasingly diversified manufacturing center; it is also the cultural capital of the Bengali-speaking people of eastern India. Its cosmopolitan population embraces skilled Sikh workers from Punjab, businessmen from Rajasthan and Gujarat on the western side of India, highly educated civil service professionals from Kerala and Madras in the south and Hindu-speaking bearers and laborers from neighboring states; the population also includes native Bengali Moslems as well as the dominant Bengali Hindu population (whose numbers have been swelled since 1947 by the influx of 700,000 refugees from East Pakistan). Calcutta is thus the scene of a major confrontation between the enduring institutions of old India—her caste communities and diversity of ethnic heritages—and the pressures and values arising from the process of urbanization that presages India's industrial revolution. What happens in Calcutta will strongly determine the character and tempo of that revolution throughout the entire country. The same can be said, in all likelihood, about the roles that are to be played by the metropolises of the other developing countries.

In Calcutta the collision of the traditional society with the forces compelling urbanization and industrialization is harsher by virtue of the fact that the city possesses no more than the rudiments of the technological apparatus that makes life possible for the comparable population and population density of London (eight million people in 693 square miles) or New York (eight million people in 365 square miles). Approaching Calcutta by air, one is struck by the almost absolute flatness of the wet delta land on which the city is spread. A network of dark green trees and waving coconut palms defines the abandoned meanders of rivers, interspersed with innumerable shallow ponds. The rest of the countryside offers nothing to one's sight that is either new or healthy. Poverty-stricken villages consisting of neglected hovels (which Mahatma Gandhi once described as "dung heaps") huddle together with increasing density up to the uncertain limits of the city. There, except for a number of industrial buildings, the structures are almost all old and often decrepit. The congestion of buildings within the city becomes heaviest at the banks of the Hooghly River, particularly at each end of the Howrah bridge. The wharf roofs and the factories stretch like a broad, dirty ribbon for miles up- and downstream from the heart of the metropolis.

On the ground the shanties made of castaway materials that crowd the road from the airport at Dum-Dum and the stench of uncovered surface drains introduce the visitor to the condition of life of the vast majority of the city's inhabitants. More than three-fourths of the population of the city of Calcutta proper live in overcrowded tenement and bustee (slum) quarters. According to an official estimate "two-thirds of the people live in kutcha (unbaked brick) buildings. More than 57 percent of multimember families have one room to live in. For more than half of the families cramped into one-room quarters there is only 30 square feet or less per family member." One study showed that the indigent in the bustees share a single water tap among 25.6 to 30.1 persons and a single latrine among 21.1 to 23.

Should the visitor have the chance to enter any of the older tenements he will be struck by the tremendous contrast that exists between what is public and what is private. The dwellings are clean and tidy inside, although they may be overcrowded. On the other hand, all the garbage and all the refuse of living and of workshops (8.6 percent of the rooms in bustees are either partly or wholly places of work) are dumped, not in stated spots or at stated times, but everywhere and at any time along the streets and lanes. Correspondingly there is no stated schedule for the collection of refuse. At all hours of the day servants throw rubbish into the streets, and no one makes it his business to complain or to mend things so that the neighborhood can remain clean.

This dreary picture is not true of every part of Calcutta. In the new residential areas of Alipore, Ballygunge and Tollygunge in the southern part of the city and in the old Esplanade quarter at the eastern side of the great central green of the maidan, life is considerably brighter for those who are economically more fortunate. And the public buildings that flank the maidan still carry an air of provincially imperial splendor, as befits a former seat of the British viceroy.

Even in the midst of the central commercial and banking districts of the city, however, the traffic situation is appalling. On an average day 500,000 pedestrians and 30,000 vehicles will cross the Howrah bridge, and the traffic jams at both ends are constant. There are never enough taxis or buses. The progress these vehicles make through the streets is slowed by the rickshaws, which are patronized generously by the citizens of Calcutta, and by the numerous carts drawn by oxen, water buffaloes or men. Foreigners complain wrongly of the sacred cows or bulls that graze from garbage bin to garbage bin in every part of town, including the central commercial districts. The cattle that interfere with traffic are far less numerous than the human beasts of burden whose lifework is to carry heavy loads on their heads or haul them in carts.

In their struggle to survive the men have driven the animals from the city. As an acquaintance of mine once remarked: "It is dearer to maintain cattle in Calcutta; one has to pay rent for stabling them, and when they die it is all loss to the owner. But a coolie can be hired without the charge of stabling him, and when he dies he dies at his own expense."

The impression is widely held that Calcutta is the center of a population "implosion," that the city is being engulfed by a tide of in-migration from the country around it. Although some such process can be said to have contributed to the city's growth in the past, this is not the case today. In an admirable demographic and economic survey of Calcutta, the Registrar General of India, Asok Mitra, observes: "It seems incredible that, while West Bengal's population grew by 33 percent in the last decade, Calcutta's should have grown by only 8 percent. In the same period Greater Bombay grew by about 39 percent. . . . The truth of the matter is indeed a paradox: that in spite of the squalor, the crowds, the swarming streets and pathways, the bustees bursting and spilling around, Calcutta is not growing fast enough."

The stagnation of Calcutta is of more than municipal concern. As Mitra contends, Calcutta is not only the capital of Bengal; it is "India's city." In 1959–1960, 25 percent of all the gross weight of cargo imported into the country and 42 percent of all exports cleared through the port of Calcutta. The city is the port of entry to those regions of India that possess the greatest concentration of industrial resources—in particular the coal and iron deposits of West Bengal, Bihar and Orissa—and thus occupy a central place in the succession of Five Year Plans advanced by the government of India. Mitra observes: "It is this fact of nature added to the richness of the hinterland and the skill of local manpower that persuaded the World Bank, the International Development Association, the Development Loan Fund and other bodies to make enormous investments of over Rs 2,500 million [or $500 million] since 1949. . . . No less than 37 projects in Bihar and West Bengal committed in the Third Plan will depend in some way on the port city of Calcutta, the total of their foreign exchange component alone running to the tidy sum of Rs 3,745 million [$750 million] at current prices. These exclude projects in Orissa which, too, depend more on Calcutta than on any other port."

By 1960 it was clear that no aspect of Calcutta's development was keeping pace with the needs of its population or its hinterland. Overcrowding, health hazards from grossly inadequate water supply and sanitation, deficiencies in the transportation system, plus deterioration of the port attendant on silting of the Hooghly —all were hampering the economic growth of India's most rapidly expanding industrial region. The government of West Bengal in 1961 created the Calcutta Metropolitan Planning Organization (CMPO) with the statutory directive of seeking the coordinated development of the entire metropolitan district. To assist in this ambitious enterprise experts have been enlisted from the United Nations technical agencies and consultants have been provided on grants from the Ford Foundation. One of the first achievements of the CMPO was the delineation of the 400 square miles of the district itself, although the jurisdiction of the organization is not limited to this region. At the outset the planners set themselves two tasks: the institution of immediate "action" programs and the framing of long-range plans that look to the needs of the city and its hinterland a generation hence.

Under the heading of action, measures are being taken to cure the situation defined in 1959 by consultants from the World Health Organization: "In India the region of endemic cholera falls mainly within the state of West Bengal, with its nucleus in greater Calcutta and dominantly in the bustee population, ill-provided with even elementary sanitation facilities." The city has had a dual water system: an intermittent and inadequately distributed supply of filtered water and a continuous supply of unfiltered water available at hydrants for street cleaning, fire fighting and flushing latrine tanks. All over the city hundreds of thousands of people are driven to use the latter source, and worse ones, every day for laundering, bathing, cooking and drinking. The interim action agenda seeks "the virtual elimination of endemic cholera through execution of the environmental program relating to water supply and the disposal of human wastes."

These measures also constitute the essence of the "slum improvement" efforts to which the planners are committed in lieu of the slum-clearance projects that characterize urban development and renewal programs elsewhere in the world [see "The Uses of Land in Cities," by Charles Abrams, page 122]. For the same gross expenditure that might rehouse 7,000 people it is estimated that present bustee quarters can be made more safely habitable for 70,000 people. With a target date of 1971, coinciding with the end of the Fourth Five Year Plan, the interim action program also calls for projects to develop low-cost housing and open new areas of habitation in the metropolitan district for 550,-000 people; to relieve traffic conditions in the city with another bridge across the Hooghly and a mass transit system; to build enough schools and train enough teachers to bring 100 percent of the children of primary school age and 60 percent of the children of secondary school age into the classroom, and to enlist "participation of the people in upgrading their own surroundings even while government services are being improved."

Outside the metropolitan district the long-range studies embrace still larger areas affected by Calcutta's development, or lack of it. The first of these is the so-called Calcutta Metropolitan Area of 4,000 square miles, on which the city depends for its daily food supplies. Beyond is the Metropolitan Region, in which the planners contemplate the development of "countermagnet" centers, such as the projected satellite port 70 miles downstream at Haldia, to draw population pressure from the center. Finally there is the Resource Region: the 500,000 square miles of country (comprising Assam, Nagaland, Manipur, Tripura and the North East Frontier Agency, as well as Bhutan, Sikkim and Nepal to the north and the states west and south of West Bengal) for all of which Calcutta is the gateway to the world. By 1986, the planners hope, the Calcutta metropolitan district will have resumed a proper rate of growth with respect to the region it serves. It must then be able to accommodate a population of 9.8 to 11.5 million, provide on the order of 5.1 million jobs (an additional 2.4 million over 1960) and have 3,900 new primary schools and 2,100 new secondary schools in operation.

For the sake of these worthy aims it would be helpful to understand now why the economic growth of Calcutta has been lagging. The cause undoubtedly lies largely in the economic situation of India as a whole. The difficulty also arises, however, from causes nearer to home. Economists and political scientists frequently express the opinion that the causes are cultural, namely that it is the conservative character of the Indian people—their other-worldliness and fatalism—that hinders the economic and social progress of the country. There may or may not be some truth in this diagnosis. It would perhaps be better to set aside speculation and start with examination of the actual situation in Calcutta. We shall ask how far life in this city—the stirring together under the most straitened material circumstances of peoples from all over India— has brought the dissolution of the old social and cultural ties they brought with them to the city. In more formal language, the question is to what degree the process of urbanization has brought increased mobility of occupation and corresponding social mobility and therewith closer integration of the components forming the society of the city. "The challenge," says a hortatory pamphlet published by the CMPO, "is not just to build some satellite towns and new houses, or to lay roads and sewer lines, but to direct the forces that govern the life and living of the people and set new values for them."

The examination begins necessarily with consideration of the role of caste in India. Caste has set the pattern of life in India since time out of memory and continues to organize the relations of people in the 570,000 villages in which 80 percent of the nation's 450 million people dwell. In the simplistic picture of the four layers of caste—the Brahman, the priest and teacher; the Kshatriya, the warrior; the Vaisya, engaged in economic pursuits, and the Sudra, the tiller and cultivator, plus the "suppressed" peoples now grouped in the so-called Scheduled Castes—it is often overlooked that caste was a way of organizing production. The system fostered a much more fine-grained texture of communities, numbering perhaps 12,000 in the country as a whole, each identified with an occupation and maintained by intramarriage. Competition was deliberately discouraged by caste. These hereditary guilds theoretically enjoyed a monopoly in the particular trades into which they had drifted within a distinct geographical region. Their occupations were ritually graded into high and low and kept ritually distant from one another. Even within the compass of small villages castes may occupy different quarters, and caste identity will tie fellow caste members from distant villages more closely together than does their daily life with fellow villagers. Yet the castes were traditionally bound by mutual ties of exchange of goods and services.

The caste communities were often distinguishable from one another by differences in custom or culture. Such differences were not suppressed but were even encouraged to exist in their own right. Hinduism thus became a federation of many local or communal cultures, all of which professed ultimate allegiance, however, to the philosophical monism represented by the Vedanta. The caste system thereby helped to lend stability to the ancient economy of agriculture and handicrafts. It provided a superstructure that evoked inner unities, instead of suppressing cultural differences in favor of uniformity.

Its teeming millions bring to Calcutta not only this diversity of heritage but also diversities with still deeper ethnic roots in language, religious faith and historical tradition. Although Bengali, Hindi and Oriya (the language of Orissa) are Indo-European languages, they are as different as French, Italian and German, and Tamil (the language of Madras) belongs to another distinctly different genus. The Sikhs are reformed Hindus; the Rajasthanis are either orthodox Hindus or belong to the Jain sect, which denies the authority of the Vedas and goes back at least to the sixth century B.C.; the Moslems, of course, embrace Islam.

The Bengali Hindus were first in residence in Calcutta. Among them the British East India Company found ready partners in commerce and allies in politics against the Mogul empire that dominated the north of India in the 17th century. The city was founded late in the century as a fortified trading post, near a village called Kali-Kata, and people were attracted from the ancient river ports lying farther upstream on the Hooghly by the prospect of trade and employment. Mercantile castes, such as the Gandhabanik (spice merchants) and Subarnabanik (bankers and traders in gold), were followed by upper-caste Brahmans and Kayasthas (scribes), who came to seek their fortune in this growing center of commerce. The East India Company's warships and troops also provided protection, which was not available from the decaying Mogul rule, against the Bargi and Mahratta raiders who harassed the countryside.

Through the 18th and 19th centuries and into the 20th the population of the city has been increased by intermittent migration from the villages and towns of Bengal. Particularly in recent years, however, these migrations have not been prompted by the "dual spur of specialization and cooperation of labor" cited by Hans

Blumenfeld in the preceding chapter as the cause of "a great wave of migration from country to city all over the globe." At the end of the 19th century agriculture in the Bengal districts surrounding Calcutta came on desperate times. The ancient irrigation system that had excited the admiration of European travelers in the 17th century had long since fallen into decay; the countryside was ravaged by repeated epidemics of malaria until the disease became endemic and the majority of the population suffered chronic infection. Those who could afford it sought refuge in the growing city of Calcutta, in the slender hope that life might be easier there. At least the chances for medical treatment, employment and education seemed better there than in the villages, which had lost their economic vitality.

Since 1947, when the British government quit India and Bengal was partitioned between India and Pakistan, strife has divided Hindu and Moslem on both sides of the new border. With each outbreak of violence Hindu villagers and townspeople of East Pakistan, whether peasants or traders, have been fleeing to Calcutta and its environs.

Today Bengalis make up half of the population of Calcutta. For them, more than for any other ethnic group, the city is "home"; the average Bengali family of 5.4 members exceeds in size the average family in the city. The Bengalis used to maintain the old "native" quarter of the city, north of the maidan, as a distinctly Bengali quarter. There are now distinguishable concentrations of Bengali-speaking Hindus in every ward of the city. Their places of residence, however, still serve in a feeble and progressively changing way to distinguish them by caste, by origin and by occupation and reflect their economic and social evolution in the course of Calcutta's history.

Among the Bengali Hindus who remain identified with the old native quarter are the Subarnabanik bankers. They have had their own moneylending businesses ever since they came to the city. In the 19th century they also thrived as commercial agents of many British firms; some invested their earnings in the shipping trade and in indigo and jute factories. They also made large investments in Calcutta real estate. In accordance with their mercantile preference for high liquidity, however, they treated such property as a commodity, for ready sale or purchase.

Down to the present day the members of this community are engaged largely in banking, insurance and real estate, with considerable holdings also in the jute, coal and textile industries. Few of them have drifted into the professions, as so many members of latter generations of wealthy families do in Western countries. Fewer still have turned up in the lower ranks of white-collar workers—a fact that bespeaks the mutual concern and protection that caste members in general afford to one another. Some distinguished scholars and writers have come from among them, but not in the same proportion as from the Brahmans and Kayasthas.

The Kansari, or brassworker, caste shows a comparable continuity of identity and residence in one ward in the northern part of the city and one ward in the south. For centuries the brass water jars, cooking pots and eating bowls that are the work of such artisans have constituted the principal imperishable possessions of the Hindu household. In recent years, however, their trade has suffered by serious competition from cheap enamel and aluminum ware and by the increasing use of glass and porcelain in the Bengali households of the city. Yet in the older Kansari ward in the north of the city there are still a large number of families who continue to make their living by something akin to their traditional calling. Some of the Kansaris in the southern ward have become goldsmiths or silversmiths, and others have taken up the making of electrical products and surgical instruments. What is notable is that members of this caste have tried to remain as close as possible to their hereditary "monopoly," with a minimum degree of adaptation or change.

From the very beginning of the city's history the upper-caste Brahmans and Kayasthas were closely associated with the British as commercial agents. As a result they were among the principal beneficiaries of the Permanent Settlement of 1793. By this dispensation Lord Cornwallis (associated with the Battle of Yorktown in American memory) set a fixed rate of assessment on productive land, in place of the sliding scale in vogue in the past. The office of zamindar—the hereditary office of revenue collector to which was attached also a property interest in the land—thereupon became a more reliably profitable one. Many well-to-do upper-caste families invested in zamindaris, or landholdings.

By virtue of their close association with the British the Bengali Brahmans and Kayasthas soon recognized the desirability of Western education. Their sons found ready berths in mercantile houses and in administrative services, not only in Bengal but all over India, where educated Bengalis followed in the wake of British administrators. By the same token, it may be said, these Bengali castes were the first to articulate the spirit of modern India. Raja Rammohun Roy, the scion of an ancient Brahman family, sought early in the 19th century to root in India the Western rational and scientific attitude; the Brahmo Samaj movement he founded gave the nation a major quotient of its intellectual leadership, numbering among its recent heirs the great Rabindranath Tagore and three of the five Bengalis who are Fellows of the Royal Society of London.

The descendants of the Brahman and Kayastha zamindars have tended to follow the Western pattern of drift into the learned professions, letters and science and into the civil service and accountancy. Their families continue to be identified with the old native quarter of Calcutta, where they are numerous and influential. Some still have wealth derived from landholdings. The statutory abolition of zamindari in the land reforms that came with Indian independence, however, has seriously depreciated this economic base. And the social preeminence of the upper-caste Bengalis has been diluted, along with that of the Bengali Hindu community as a whole, by the huge influx of poverty-stricken Hindu refugees from East Pakistan. Nonetheless, the Bengalis in general dominate the middle-income group of the city. Whereas they constitute half of the population of Calcutta, they make up more than three-quarters of the city's middle class.

The eastern and northeastern fringes of Calcutta, where the land is low and even now subject to flooding, were initially inhabited by Bengali fisherfolk and gardeners supplying the numerous markets of the city. They usually belonged to Scheduled Castes (the former "untouchables"). Some of them lived in separate settlements of their own, among more prosperous neighbors. Many of these low-caste people have lost their hereditary occupational identity and have joined the ranks of either skilled or unskilled labor. In recent years those who have had the advantage of education have become indistinguishable from their upper-caste neighbors in the matter of livelihood. The numbers of the Bengali poor have been swelled by the refugees from East Pakistan; they belong to many different castes but have a social identity of their own. Generally speaking, the Bengalis are to be found in all quarters of the city, providing a Bengali matrix in which other ethnic groups assert their identity.

Just as the better-off Bengalis dominate the middle class, so the poor Bengalis constitute three-quarters of Calcutta's unemployed. The Bengali family man, for whom Calcutta is home, today finds himself at a disadvantage in the contest for jobs in the sluggish economy of the city. Half of the "households"—spending and earning "economic units"—in the city are simply single men. The ratio of male to female in the population is 60 to 40. These extraordinary facts of the city's demography reflect the presence in the city of tens of thousands of lone males who have come in search of work. They come with the hope of earning a little more than enough to keep body and soul together and so being able to send money home to their families in their native villages.

The largest numbers come from Uttar Pradesh and Bihar. Both Moslems and Hindus, they speak Hindi, the statutory "national" language of India. These men live singly or in "messing groups" of five or so in the tenements and slums of the northern, eastern and southern reaches of the city, where they provide the bulk of the labor employed in the factories located in these wards. Some live also in the commercial wards and work in the carrying trades, pushing and pulling handcarts and carrying sacks and baskets on their heads. In these ranks should be counted also the Oriya-speaking workers from Orissa.

Their skimping and saving builds up bigger balances in the postal savings accounts in Calcutta than in any other city in India in spite of the relatively low wages in the jute mills, and their postal money orders go out to the villages at a higher value per order. In the effort to achieve this heroic transfer of income, Mitra says, these workers get along "without the barest minimum of housing, sanitation, comfort and privacy." The figures also indicate that a large part of the income produced in Calcutta is not available for expenditure in the city.

At the other end of the social scale the Bengali middle class sustains corresponding competition from ethnic groups that are not as deeply rooted in the city. When Bengalis emerged in the first quarter of this century as spokesmen for the national independence movement, the British commercial and ruling classes sought to replace their Bengali subordinates whenever there was a chance to do so. Members of Rajasthani commercial castes came forward in the economy of Calcutta at this time. It was not until after independence, however, that the large Rajasthani element in the trade and commerce of the city began to regard it as their home. They have entered into industry as well as into foreign commerce; they are remodeling their old business organizations on British lines and taking over establishments from the departing British. The Rajasthani families are sending their sons to British schools, and they are moving from their enclaves in the old native quarter north of the maidan to the more spacious and openly prosperous wards in the south. So strong is their position in the business community that they have renamed their trade association the "Indian Chamber of Commerce."

These developments might not have had much significance if the economy of Calcutta were thriving. Nor would they be felt so strongly if separate economic interests were not identified with groups distinguished from one another by ethnic differences as well. As things stand, relative change in economic fortunes gives cultural differences an undesirable significance. In a memorandum to the government of West Bengal the Bengal Trade Association complained that Bengali traders as well as the Bengali "middle-class salariat" were being discriminated against in the transfer of British concerns to Indian (predominantly non-Bengali) hands. The memorandum also complained that a large number of Bengalis who were graduated from technical institutions are unable to find adequate employment. How far these statements were objectively true is beside the point. The fact is that feelings of this kind corrode intercommunal sentiment in a city where poverty threatens and presses on people from all around.

The business and commercial classes include a group of traders that came originally from Gujarat and has ties to powerful interests in Bombay. These Gujaratis have been in residence in Calcutta for three generations and have been engaged in the textile, timber and tobacco trades. They have also put capital into the coal and shipping industries. As they have prospered they have come to dominate one ward in the south from which the original Bengali residents have progressively moved away.

The Punjabis in Calcutta can be broadly divided into two groups: the Sikhs, who are largely in the transportation business, and others who are in commerce and large-scale industry. They live mostly in the southern wards that have been attracting the better-off. The South Indians—from Andhra Pradesh, Madras, Mysore and Kerala—fill white-collar jobs, from high administrative to lowly clerical, in government and business offices. They do not regard themselves as permanent residents of the city, but they nonetheless have established their own neighborhoods in several wards in the more suburban districts to the south.

Calcutta has a relatively large Christian community, including Europeans (who once formed its upper class) and Anglo-Indians, Goanese with Portuguese ancestors and Indians (who form its middle and lower classes). As might be expected, they inhabit the former European section of the city. This is a set of contiguous wards around the south and east of the maidan and the central office district. Europeans formerly occupied the uppermost levels of the city's social hierarchy. They lived in palatial houses with large gardens and open spaces, which they owned or rented from Bengali landlords. Their residences are now being bought by Rajasthanis, Punjabis and other prosperous non-Bengalis. Anglo-Indians and Indian Christians used to be employed, under European patronage, in the railways, docks and commercial establishments. Today the Indian Christians are indistinguishable from, say, other Bengalis if they are Bengali-speaking. The Anglo-Indians have been migrating away from the city and even from India.

The Moslem population, although it is not fractionated by caste, is quite explicitly stratified by class. Two large Moslem quarters surround the places of residence in the southwest and south of the city that were furnished by the East India Company to the Nawab of Oudh and the descendants of the Tippoo Sultan of Mysore. The Moslem middle-class commercial people live in wards near the central business district; the lower-class Moslems live in the tenement and slum districts of the east and northeast and in large tracts of the city surrounding the old centers of the Moslem aristocracy in the south and southwest. Many lower-class Moslems used to be employed in the soap and leather industries—

regarded among Hindus as polluting occupations and reserved to "low"-caste people.

The map of Calcutta thus shows a highly differentiated texture. Ethnic groups tend to cluster together in their own quarters. They are distinguished from one another not only by language and culture but also by broad differences in the way they make their living. Naturally there is a considerable amount of overlap, but this does not obscure the fact that each ethnic group tends to pursue a particular range of occupations.

It can be said, therefore, that the diverse ethnic groups in the population of the city have come to bear the same relation to one another as do the castes in India as a whole. They do not enjoy monopoly of occupation, as under caste, nor are they tied to one another by tradition in reciprocal exchange of goods and services. There is also no ritual grading of occupation into high and low. But preference for or avoidance of some kinds of work are expressed in class differences among occupations, as can be observed elsewhere in the world. The social order of Calcutta might therefore seem to be evolving through a transitional stage, in which caste is being replaced by an increasingly distinct class system.

Actually, the superstructure that coheres the castes under the old order seems instead to be reestablishing itself in a new form. Calcutta today is far from being a melting pot on the model of cities in the U.S. There the Irish, Italian and eastern European immigrants have merged their identities within a few generations. The communal isolation of the first generations was quickly reduced by occupational mobility in the expanding American economy and by the uniform system of public education that Americanized their children.

In Calcutta the economy is an economy of scarcity. Because there are not enough jobs to go around everyone clings as closely as possible to the occupation with which his ethnic group is identified and relies for economic support on those who speak his language, on his coreligionists, on members of his own caste and on fellow immigrants from the village or district from which he has come. By a backwash, reliance on earlier modes of group identification reinforces and perpetuates differences between ethnic groups.

The respect that has traditionally been shown to cultural dif-

ferences under caste has also played some part in maintaining the
segregation of ethnic groups. Although Calcutta is the center of
Bengali culture, a Bengali wishes a Rajasthani to remain as he is
rather than demand that he conform to the ways of Bengalis. Calcutta has numerous schools in which the language of instruction
is Hindi, Urdu, Gujarati or Oriya. The state government does not
insist on imposing the Bengali language in the schools, and this has
been the policy of the University of Calcutta ever since its found-
ing in 1857.

One would think that the new types of urban occupation and
common concern for besetting civic problems might tend to bring
integration of the ethnic groups through voluntary organization.
Such is not the case. A careful study of these organizations has
disclosed that language groups so far have come together only at
two levels of enterprise. One is at the top of the hierarchy, represented by the Calcutta Club or the Rotary Club. The other is
in the labor unions, where workmen from different cultural backgrounds do unite to promote their collective interests. Otherwise
the large number of voluntary organizations in the city, run for
purposes of education, mutual aid or recreation, are ethnically
more or less exclusive.

Such imperfect urbanization in an economy of scarcity under-
lies the tensions among ethnic groups that now and then come
divisively to the surface. The situation heavily conditions the prospects of success of the ambitious program of the Metropolitan
Planning Organization. Even if Calcutta begins in the near future
to offer many new opportunities for employment, communal tensions are likely to be a feature of the city's life for a considerable
period to come.

On the other hand, it may be hoped that progress need not bring
a leveling of all cultural differences to the drab uniformity of so
many great cities of the West. Regard for ways of life other than
one's own has been a central theme of Hindu civilization. This
value may perhaps be reaffirmed in new ways and in new institutions, in spite of the impatience and intolerance that characterize
the present urban age. In all probability the economic, social and
cultural changes so ardently desired for the welfare of the people
of Calcutta can take place only as a result of such a resolve of the
mind and spirit.

Stockholm:
A Planned City

· GÖRAN SIDENBLADH

The concept of planning the development of a city came late to most cities. Stockholm is an exception: its growth has been planned since the establishment of a city planning office more than 300 years ago.

THE CITY OF STOCKHOLM stands on a group of islands and fingers of mainland at the edge of the Baltic Sea. It is a city of palaces, ancient dwellings, parks, waterways, many bridges (42 at the latest count) and magnificent architecture, most notably exemplified by the tower of its famous Town Hall, which was built between 1911 and 1923. Like other old European cities, Stockholm is a mixture of many styles: narrow lanes and broad boulevards, age-grimed houses and modern apartments, mansard roofs and glass skyscrapers. Yet among the world's old cities Stockholm bears a unique distinction. It did not just grow: from the beginning of its modern history it has been to some degree a planned city.

Stockholm was founded as a fortress in the 13th century by an early ruler of the Swedish kingdom, Birger Jarl. It grew slowly as a port in the Middle Ages, but it did not become an important city until King Gustavus Adolphus and his successors established it as Sweden's national capital in the 17th century. Its career as a planned city began at that time. This early interest in planning came about primarily through the force of accident. A primitive city built mainly of wood, Stockholm throughout its early centuries was repeatedly damaged by great fires; in the century beginning in 1640, for instance, its southern area suffered eight conflagrations that burned down whole parishes within a day or two. Compelled to rebuild, the city turned its disasters into opportunity by undertaking to build according to orderly plans. Its governing officials appointed a city planner, called "conductor." This city planning office, now nearly 330 years old, has been in charge of designing the development of Stockholm ever since.

As early as 1640 the city adopted master plans for the growth of the areas that were then suburbs. Within the past 100 years it has carried out a series of plans that have transformed it from a modest-sized capital to a major metropolis. Metropolitan Stockholm has advanced from a population of barely 100,000 a century ago to more than 1.2 million today. It is now growing at the rate of about 2 percent a year; the rise amounts to about half of Sweden's total annual population increase.

Stockholm's ability to plan its physical, economic and social development must be attributed mainly to one all-important factor: public ownership of the land. If destructive fires in the city made planning necessary, government control of the land made it possible. This tradition of land control has a long history.

Before the 19th century there was almost no such thing as private ownership of land in large parts of Stockholm. The lands belonged either to the crown or to the city. The owner of a house paid a ground fee for the use of the land on which it stood. The fee might be only nominal, to be sure, but it served to establish that the land did not belong to the user. In Stockholm the governor of the city could tell the owner of a building to move it to another site, and he could offer sites in new subdivisions to any who were willing and able to build on them. This was, indeed, the basis of the first master plan of 1640. Home builders and others were provided with land on condition that they put them to the stipulated use and build within a stipulated period.

In the course of time, however, the ground-fee system was whittled away. Those who had erected permanent buildings were allowed to buy full title to the land for a sum amounting to about

30 times the annual ground fee. By 1850 much of the land area of Stockholm had passed into private ownership. Consequently, when the city officials sought to put into effect new master plans adopted in 1866, they found that the necessary acquisition of land made some of their projects very costly. A new building code for the city, allowing the erection of multistory apartment dwellings, had raised land values. The city, wishing to build wide boulevards on the Paris model, found itself limited in the ability to do so.

Today Stockholm, in carrying out redevelopment plans for the inner city, must resort to the strategy of land purchase that is becoming familiar in urban renewal programs in the U.S. The city buys up a block of land—not only the parcels required for streets and other public improvements but also the area that is to be re-developed for commercial and housing areas. Under the Swedish Building Act the private owners are required to sell at the actual market value. Because the land prices tend to jump when a plan for development of an area has been adopted, the city persuaded the Swedish Riksdag (Parliament) to enact an amendment that enables the city to acquire the land it needs for renewal before it has settled on a specific plan. This amendment, passed in 1953, has proved to be of basic importance in keeping land prices within reason. After the city has acquired ownership, it retains control over the increment in land value by leasing, rather than selling, the cleared land to the new developers. When the present renewal programs have been completed, the Stockholm government expects to end up as owner of more than half of the central business area.

As other chapters in this book indicate, modern city planning begins with analysis of the city's economic functions. The economic history of Stockholm can be summed up very briefly. Until a century or so ago the city functioned mainly as the center of Sweden's government—the king's court, the parliament and their attendant departments—and as a port for trade with countries around the Baltic. With the advent of the industrial revolution Stockholm became an important industrial center. Stockholm still contains more manufacturing industry than any other city in the nation. As in most other large cities, however, its economic base is now rapidly changing. In the 1950's the main growth of industry was in other centers in Sweden; the number of workers employed

in manufacturing increased more than twice as fast in the rest of
the country as it did in Stockholm. The capital city is now con-
centrating more and more on the service industries that characterize the world's metropolises [see "The Modern Metropolis," by
Hans Blumenfeld, page 40].

Folke Kristensson of the Stockholm School of Economics has
grouped the services in Stockholm into five categories. The first
consists of the policy-making headquarters of large industrial organizations and other major enterprises, the various special services
catering to these institutions and the main centers of retail trade:
big department stores, specialty shops and the like. The second
category includes large business organizations that provide services
of a routine kind less closely associated with policy making, and
small industrial enterprises that are still in the experimental stage
or at least not yet ready for large-scale production; also put in this
category are universities and other research centers. The third
category is made up of materials-handling industries—associated
with shipping—that require large waterfront areas. The fourth
category is large-scale manufacturing, which now tends to be
located on the fringes of the metropolitan area. The fifth category is the complex of consumer services (shops, schools and so
on) that are localized in residential districts. As living standards
rise, more people are employed in these consumer services; they
now account for about 20 percent of the total working population of metropolitan Stockholm.

Obviously no city plan can exercise direct control over the
forces that determine economic and population growth. Indirectly,
however, sound and imaginative planning can have a great deal of
influence. By making the metropolis an attractive place to live and
by offering desirable sites to business, a good plan can be a big help
in promoting a city's development. Of course, much also depends
on the policies of the national government. In Sweden the government influences building activities by providing national building loans, by issuing permits for commercial buildings (through
the National Labor Board), by requiring cities to get government
permission to borrow money for public building and by financing
the construction of the principal arterial highways. During and
immediately after World War II the Swedish government used its
powers to direct industrial development into depressed areas of

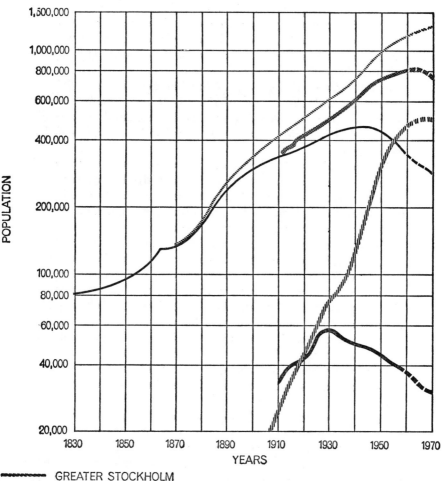

POPULATION

1,500,000
1,000,000
800,000
600,000
400,000
200,000
100,000
80,000
60,000
40,000
20,000

1830 1850 1870 1890 1910 1930 1950 1970

YEARS

GREATER STOCKHOLM
CITY OF STOCKHOLM
INNER CITY
SUBURBS
CENTER RESIDENTIAL AREA

POPULATION TRENDS of the Stockholm area are charted logarithmically.
Greater Stockholm includes the entire metropolitan area.

threatening unemployment. In recent years it has followed the policy of encouraging the movement of people into areas that need workers. These areas are primarily the regions around the three large cities in the southern part of the country, and at present there is heavy migration to these centers.

In the light of this survey of Stockholm's history and background, let us look at some of the recent and present planning activities in the city. We shall start with the central business district, to which a large part of our attention has been devoted in recent years.

The central islands of Stockholm contain many of the city's oldest and best-known institutions, but the islands constitute only a comparatively small part of the total central area. The main business district lies on the mainland, forming the northern part of the inner city. Around the turn of the century it became evident that drastic renewal was necessary for this area. Its business buildings, many of them multistory stone dwellings that had been converted to commercial use, were overdue for replacement by more efficient structures. The streets were narrow and congested. A high ridge ran down the middle of the district, producing hilly streets that could be climbed by a horse but that were too steep for the new powered vehicles just coming in. The city therefore started a program of improving traffic by making deep cuts through the ridge to produce level streets. The first of these new east-west avenues—Kungsgatan (King's Street)—was opened in 1911.

In 1912 the city officials approved detailed plans for further redevelopment of the business area. The city began to buy up properties for this purpose, but prices were high and progress was slow. In any event, it was finally realized that the 1912 plan would be obsolete before it could be put into effect. In 1932 an international competition was held for the best solution to the problems of the area. Altogether about 350 plans were submitted, but the only result was intensified arguments among the aldermen and other officials in the city hall.

Stockholm is governed by an elected city assembly with 100 members representing four political parties (Social Democrats, Liberals, Conservatives and Communists). Among the aldermen are nine who head one or more commissions having charge of specific city functions. By 1940 the planning commission was under a Liberal alderman; the finance and "real estate" commissions were under Social Democrats. In addition to party rivalries there were conflicting views of the various plans within the parties themselves. The debates went on right through World War II. At length, in 1945, the city assembly agreed on a broad plan, and a more detailed plan was presented in 1946. For several years, however, no actual work was started. The political and administrative problems were finally solved in 1951 when the assembly delegated full responsibility for preparing plans to a committee composed of the various aldermen and representatives of other interests involved. This committee obtains the views of businessmen and the public, through newspaper discussion and other means, before it approves a project.

The 1946 plan was amended and expanded as time went on. A shopping mall for pedestrians, from which vehicular traffic is barred, has been built in the center of the commercial district. Underground passages are provided for the unloading of trucks in the business area. At busy corners there will be underground crossings, with escalators, for pedestrians. Some narrow streets have been widened; others are closed to vehicles between 11:00 A.M. and midnight. For through traffic there will be bypasses on the western and northern sides of the business district and a tunnel from southwest to northeast.

In 1962 the city approved a revised and extended renewal plan that will clear a considerable part of the business section and devote a fourth of the cleared area to new streets, a fourth to multilevel parking garages and the remaining half to new commercial buildings. The program will cost about two billion Swedish crowns (approximately $400 million), of which a fifth will be supplied through public funds for the traffic improvements and four-fifths will be invested by private sources in the new buildings. The renewal area involves some 800 pieces of property. Of these 120 have already been renewed, and about half of the remaining 680 have been or will be acquired by the city. Many of those not to be taken over are in such condition that it is believed the owners themselves may want to pull them down or sell them for renewal.

In housing its people Stockholm has made greater strides than in

renewal ⸢f the business center. This is due principally to the foresight of the city fathers, who early in the century began to buy
outlying land for expansion of the city's suburbs. As a result the
development of most of the outer residential areas has proceeded
in planned and orderly fashion. Indeed, this phase of planning
activities by Stockholm is probably the city's most important
achievement.

In 1904 the Stockholm city assembly set out to buy large areas
of farm and forest lands outside the ancient city limits with a view
to building "garden cities" as suburbs for the metropolis. Concurrently the city extended its boundaries so that the new suburbs
came within the city limits. Some of these areas lay idle for as long
as 20 years before they were developed, but the city reaped the
benefit of having acquired them at very low cost. Unfortunately
the buying program did not go far enough; since 1916 the city has
made only one incorporation. In 1953 the parliament enacted a
law allowing cities to acquire land by condemnation so that they
could lease it at low rates for the construction of moderately
priced housing. Stockholm has invoked this law in only a few
cases, but its existence has made the purchase of land at fair prices
easier.

The general plan for Stockholm's structure in this century began
with the idea that the central area should have high density, with
a zone of multifamily housing surrounding the business center,
and the suburban region outside this zone should have uniformly
low density, consisting mainly of one-family houses. Over the
past 20 years the Stockholm planners' concept of a desirable arrangement for the suburbs has changed considerably. At the end
of World War II the influx of population to metropolitan Stockholm was much greater than had been expected, and the density
of population in the suburbs began to build up. The planners therefore proposed the development of suburban units (which may be
called "neighborhood units" or semisatellite towns). Each unit
would have its own shopping centers and cultural facilities, and
most neighborhoods would be connected to the center of the city
by extensions of the local railway system.

A master plan for development of this scheme was published
in 1952. By virtue of its powers of planning, leasing the land and
allotting loans for building, the city has been able to promote the

building of the suburban centers according to plan. By 1963 there were 18 such communities, with a total population of nearly 250,-000, and five more are under construction. Originally it was intended that each community should be limited to about 10,000 people, but this number proved to be too small to support adequate shopping facilities and cultural services. Consequently some of the neighborhoods have been planned for populations of about 25,000. Notable among these are Vällingby on the western side of the city and Farsta in the south. The latest plans have turned to a somewhat different arrangement: neighborhood units of just over 10,000 people each are grouped in clusters, with one large center of shops and services in each cluster.

A powerful influence in modifying the plans for development of the suburbs has been, of course, the automobile. In Stockholm in 1945 there were only nine private cars per 1,000 inhabitants; by the end of 1964 this figure had risen to 190 per 1,000. The increased mobility of the residents tends to make the neighborhood center less important. On the other hand, neighborhood concentration of dwellings is made increasingly essential by the problem of traveling to the center of the city. The only feasible solution to this travel problem, for most of those who must make the trip daily, is rail transport. If the railroad or subway is to be an attractive alternative to the private automobile, one should be able to live within walking distance of the railroad station. The planning rule is that suburban apartments should be within about a quarter of a mile, and single-family houses within about half a mile, of a rapid-transit station. In most of the plans made since 1950 this standard has been achieved. In other areas the gap is filled by providing connecting bus service, but this method of transportation has not proved sufficiently popular to make such bus lines an economical proposition.

One way of reducing the dimensions of the traffic problem is to decentralize employment so that a large proportion of the suburban residents can work in their own communities. Twenty years ago this objective was eagerly discussed in Stockholm. The master plan for the Vällingby suburb contemplated the construction of business and service establishments that would employ half of the workers expected to live in the area. For various reasons this goal has not been reached. By 1960 Vällingby provided jobs for some 9,000 gainfully employed persons, which corresponds to about a third of the number of wage earners (27,000) with homes in that area. But only 2,000 of those jobs were occupied by Vällingby residents; the other 7,000 workers came from other neighborhoods. Thus 7,000 workers daily commuted into Vällingby and 25,000 residents commuted out, half of them to the center of the city, 30 minutes away by subway. The proportion of Vällingby residents employed locally probably has improved since 1960, because some of the local enterprises had just opened at that time, but this does not alter the essential problem. Establishments employing mostly unskilled workers or women have considerable success in recruiting a work force locally in the suburbs; the workers in other categories, however, tend to take the entire city as their employment market and prefer to travel to where the best opportunities are located.

An industrial or service enterprise must consider many factors in deciding where to locate its establishment: not only the convenience and cost of its employees' travel to work but also its other transportation costs, the efficiency of the site for its particular purposes, the accessibility of services with which it must maintain close contact, and so on. An activity requiring highly trained and specialized workers often must be centrally located so that it can draw on the entire city's resources of skilled manpower. Nonetheless, for many types of establishment there is much to recommend location in the suburbs. For one thing, such a location facilitates the employment of married women, who are entering the labor market in growing numbers. Furthermore, the increasing ownership of cars by workers now makes it possible for a suburban center to recruit its employees from a large area.

This mobility, paradoxically, is not an unmixed blessing for retail business in the suburbs. We have found in the Stockholm area that it is difficult to keep isolated, small suburban shops alive. More and more people tend to drive to elaborate shopping centers to do their buying, passing by not only the store down the street but also the modest shopping area at the center of the unit.

Like other metropolises, Stockholm today is faced with the onrush of the automobile, which is complicating rational solution of the city's transit problems. Car ownership in the Stockholm metropolitan area is increasing at the rate of 12 percent a year. The city's physical fragmentation on 15 islands and three stretches of mainland separated by water makes auto travel particularly difficult (although many other cities have the same kinds of bottleneck). In order to reach the central business district of Stockholm by car from the western suburbs one has to cross two bridges; from the southern suburbs one must cross three. Every morning some 100,000 people (according to the 1960 statistics) come to work in the inner city from the southern suburbs alone. Private cars could not possibly deliver any such volume of traffic. As early as 1908 the city assembly realized that subways, supplementing the national railway lines, would be essential to get people into the center of the city. Construction was not actually begun until the end of World War II. The first subway system, running into the center from the western and southern suburbs and swinging around through the main parts of the business district, was completed in 1957. In 1964 a second system, running from the southwestern to the northeastern section of the city, was opened. A third system is on the drawing boards.

Each train consists of eight cars and has a total capacity of 1,100 to 1,200 passengers, with seats for 400. During rush hours the trains run on a two-minute schedule in the central area. The average travel speed is 20 miles an hour.

Stockholm has invested more than a billion Swedish crowns ($200 million) in the subways. Four-fifths of the cost of their operation is paid by revenues, and the remaining fifth out of taxes. It has now become necessary to extend the subway system outside the city limits. Early this year the Swedish parliament gave important recognition of this need for mass transportation by providing that subways be built with aid from national highway funds, raised by taxes on gasoline and automobiles. This remarkable concession gives evidence of the growing realization in all countries that for intracity travel, transport mechanisms other than the private automobile must be the main ones if our great cities are to survive.

In the popularity contest between the private car and the train, the train now runs a poor second in most places. (The bus apparently is not a generally acceptable alternative to either; running on the same highways as the private car, it shares the disadvantage of traffic congestion without having the private car's advantages.)

Can the subway or other means of rail transport compete with the car as the preferred vehicle for travel into the city? In Stockholm car owners seem to be more willing to ride the subway to work than workers in U.S. cities of about the same size. We believe the Stockholm subway system and the way we build around it will attract twice as much use of this public transport system as is now made in American cities.

In 1961 public means of transport were used by 87 percent of the riders to work in the central business district of Stockholm, by 71 percent of those traveling to work in other parts of the inner city, by 52 percent of those working in the near suburbs (within 10 miles) and by 35 percent of those in the outer suburbs. Sven Lundberg, chief of the city's traffic planning department, estimates that 15 years from now these percentages will be respectively 90, 50, 15 and 15 percent. That is to say, nearly all the people working in the center of the city will travel by subway, but most of those working in the suburbs will drive to work.

Our planning thoughts are now focused on Greater Stockholm's future growth as a metropolis. It is clear that the scope of the plans and the planning organization will have to be enlarged, because the city itself has reached the limit of the number of people it can house. Since 1930 the population of metropolitan Stockholm has increased from 600,000 to 1,250,000, and the number of dwelling rooms has been raised from 500,000 to 1,500,000; that is, while the population has doubled, new construction has trebled the amount of housing, so that each person has more living space. This expansion has been made possible by development of the suburbs. It is unlikely that the density of habitation will increase; on the contrary, it will probably be reduced to an average of .5 person per room instead of the present .8 per room. During the past 35 years housing construction in the metropolitan area has added a million rooms, and it is now continuing at the rate of 70,000 rooms, or 18,000 new dwellings, a year. If this average is maintained for the next 35 years, there will be four million dwelling rooms in the metropolis by the year 2000, enough to house a population of two million at the expected density.

Metropolitan Stockholm now has a regional planning agency whose scope includes the city proper (population 800,000) and 45 other municipalities with populations ranging from less than

1,000 to 50,000. This agency, however, has only negative powers: it can prohibit developments it does not like but cannot see to it that the right things are built in the right place at the right time. Moreover, the large municipalities in the metropolitan area are already built up nearly to their capacity. For further growth, therefore, the metropolis must expand into areas now peacefully rural. One important step toward establishing a larger planning jurisdiction has already been taken. This is the creation of a Stockholm "Metropolitan Traffic Company," which from 1967 on will be responsible for planning and coordinating all local transit and traffic arrangements within the entire region. Most probably the city of Stockholm will soon take the further step of joining the county council of the surrounding province in setting up a country-wide planning organization to handle the development of housing and other metropolitan facilities. For this purpose the city assembly may have to cede political responsibility for the overall planning to a council elected from the whole region.

Ciudad Guayana:
A New City

· LLOYD RODWIN

Venezuela is building a metropolis as a key part of a plan to advance its national economy. The effort is complicated by the fact that the impoverished residents of the countryside are "imploding" to the site.

IN THE LOWER ORINOCO VALLEY of Venezuela a new city is rising. Called Ciudad Guayana, this city is more than just another urban settlement: it is the focal point of an effort to establish the national economy of Venezuela on a broader and more stable basis than its present heavy dependence on petroleum. As such the city of Guayana is perhaps one of the most ambitious and significant enterprises of its kind in the world today. In a book about cities Ciudad Guayana provides an instructive example of the problems of planning new cities in developing countries.

At first the opportunity to build a city from the ground up may seem the answer to a planner's dream. It appears to offer a chance for maximum freedom and scope in design without the necessity of having to cope with outmoded existing development, entrenched property interests and recalcitrant attitudes of the inhabitants. Actually, as experienced planners know, such an enterprise begins with severe handicaps. It lacks at the outset the basic foundations needed for building a city: the presence of a trained force of technicians and workers, established community relations and loyalties, consumer and business services, community facilities —in short, the germinal conditions for the support and growth of the urban organism. To prepare sound plans takes time. If, as sometimes happens, work is already under way or must begin immediately, skilled specialists must be imported, housing and schools built, water and electricity supplied and transportation provided long before the plans are completed. Attracted by the prospect of jobs, poor migrants invade the area, put up makeshift shelters and exacerbate the problem of organizing land uses and public services. Most costs tend to be high, almost no amenities exist and living conditions are bleak. Understandably enough, the inhabitants become impatient with "fancy" long-range plans and delays; they grumble about the neglect of their immediate needs and care little if these needs do not fit the priorities or the plans. Up to a point their views can be slighted or ignored, but this is always dangerous. It is hardly surprising that the new city rarely measures up to the original dreams of its planners.

Nevertheless, there are several reasons why planning a new city in these circumstances is still an exciting challenge. The new city can reinforce national policies for economic growth, help transform backward regions and relieve the pressures on other cities. It may afford opportunities for boldness, imagination and innovation on a scale rarely possible elsewhere. Ciudad Guayana well exemplifies these problems and opportunities.

The location of Ciudad Guayana would hardly appear to be an inviting place to build a new city. Isolated (it is 300 miles from Caracas, the capital city), tropical in climate and generally inferior in agricultural potential, the region is dominated by vast expanses of savanna and tropical forest broken only by treacherous rivers and low mountain ranges. Sporadic discoveries of diamonds, however, combined with memories of gold mining in the 19th century, have created the myth of fabulous riches awaiting the adventurous that "Guayana" still suggests to most Venezuelans. As a result of the myth the region is unmistakably a frontier for those within it as well as those outside.

The region does have extraordinary resources. There are rich deposits of high-grade iron ore and promising possibilities for the mining of manganese, nickel, chromium, gold, industrial diamonds and perhaps bauxite and aluminum laterite. Within 60 miles of Ciudad Guayana there are large fields of petroleum and natural gas. The settlement is on the banks of the Orinoco River, which provides direct access to the ocean. Running through the heart of the city is a branch of the Orinoco, the Caroni River, which has a hydroelectric potential of about 10 million kilowatts. With an abundance of potential power, water, timber and iron ore, Ciudad Guayana is admirably equipped to be a center of industry.

As recently as 1950 the population of the area was only 4,000. Then two U.S.-owned organizations, the Orinoco Mining Company and the Iron Mines Company, built plants in Guayana for iron-ore processing and created small settlements for their staffs. Later the Venezuelan government began the construction of a large steel plant on the Orinoco a few miles west of these centers. In 1959 President Betancourt's administration, recognizing the potential of the Guayana region, created a public corporation to develop it. This agency, the Corporación Venezolana de Guayana (CVG), was entrusted with the job of devising a strategy for the development of the region. The corporation took over the steel plant, which was still under construction, and the Macagua Dam at the Caroní River falls. It also took on the job of planning the growth of the city. It acquired much of the land within the prospective city area, through purchase from private owners and through transfer of public lands from other government agencies. The powers of the corporation, however, were limited by the activities and jurisdiction of other agencies. Its capacity to act was also handicapped by shortages of skilled staff. To help overcome this limitation the CVG engaged the assistance of the Joint Center for Urban Studies of the Massachusetts Institute of Technology and Harvard University.

The site confronting the planners was an area some 15 miles long on the south side of the Orinoco. The terrain was vast and in some respects spectacular. It was dominated by the broad Orinoco, the falls of the Caroní and heights above both rivers. Scattered over this area were several disconnected settlements. At the western end was the steel plant, at the eastern end a community called San Félix. Between them were a mining town called Puerto Ordaz, built by the Orinoco Mining Company for its staff, an-

other mining settlement called Palua and various smaller developments that sprawled along connecting highways. The Caroní
River, running north-south, cut the area in two; a bridge across
it was under construction.

Logically the first task was to study the potential for economic
development of the city and formulate plans that would encourage the appropriate economic activities and related functions. Before this could be done there were pressing immediate problems.
Workers looking for jobs in this promising new industrial center
were already arriving in large numbers. By 1961 the population of
Guayana had mushroomed from 4,000 to 42,000; in 1962 it increased to 50,000; in 1964 it had risen to 70,000. The former village of San Félix alone had 45,000 inhabitants. New shantytowns
were springing up overnight. There was a clamor for housing,
water, sewers, electricity, roads, schools. Without waiting for the
completion of studies or long-range plans the planners had to find
and prepare sites for the temporary settlement of newcomers, for
low-rent housing and for industrial plants, and had to redesign
site plans that had been made earlier and public works that were
already under way in order to avoid damage to the long-range
interests of the community.

For example, one of the immediate issues was the new bridge
across the Caroní, on which work was already well advanced. It
was too late to enlarge the capacity of the bridge, which should
have been twice what it was, but the planners won a short delay
in construction that enabled them to design separate lanes for
bicycles and pedestrians so that they would not be endangered
by automobile traffic across the bridge. The local population
ardently desired the Caroní bridge. Since it was destined to be a
critical visual element and an important symbol of the future
city, the planning staff wanted to make it as meaningful for the
residents of Ciudad Guayana as the Ponte Vecchio is to the people of Florence.

The studies for a long-range plan for the city began with a detailed assessment of the role it would play in the development of
the Venezuelan economy. Over the past 25 years the country's
economy has grown at the impressive rate of 7 percent a year,
thanks largely to exploitation of its oil resources. To maintain this
growth rate and take care of the needs of the expanding popula-

tion, which is increasing at the rate of 3 percent a year, it was estimated that Venezuela would probably have to raise its output of goods and services fourfold in the next 20 years. It would be unsound to depend mainly on petroleum, particularly because this resource was bound to decline in the long run. Examination of the country's needs, potentialities and existing industries led to the conclusion that its industrial development should focus strongly on the production of metals, petrochemicals and machinery. Existing Venezuelan industries, which are largely final-assembly activities, require these basic and intermediate products. Their production would not only fill gaps in the domestic economy but also provide Venezuela with export goods for trade with other Latin-American countries and the rest of the world. The studies suggested that the country should give high priority specifically to the production of iron and steel, sponge iron, aluminum, other metals and metal products, heavy machinery, electrochemicals and forest products such as pulp and paper.

Analysis of location, cost and other factors indicated that if these activities were located in the Guayana region, they would enjoy comparative advantage and could compete successfully in foreign markets. On the basis of the many factors involved, including projections of the future demand and markets for the various products, a comprehensive program for investment in production facilities was worked out. It had two phases: a program for the period 1963 to 1966 and a follow-up plan for 1967 to 1975. Since Guayana is in a food-deficit area, the program included proposals for increasing the production of food, particularly in the area of the Orinoco delta.

Venezuela incorporated this program in its national plan. It projected a total investment of some $3.8 billion in the Guayana region over the next 10 years. Of this the Venezuelan national government itself will provide more than $500 million for the period 1965–1968 and about $1.5 billion for 1969–1975. (This amounts to roughly 10 percent of the total Venezuelan public investment in both periods.) The rest is expected to come from private capital (domestic and foreign) and from loans by international agencies. As a result of these investments it is hoped that by 1975 the Guayana region will provide about a fifth of Venezuela's total of manufacturing and export products.

This, then, yielded the first approximations of the economic prospects for Ciudad Guayana. Corrections will of course be necessary when better data become available and if some of the assumptions turn out to be erroneous. This is an inescapable hazard of planning for the future; fortunately the high-speed computer will at least speed up the chores of calculation. Meanwhile, on the basis of these projections, the planning staff worked out the implications for employment and population characteristics. The indications were that the city would have a population of close to 100,000 by 1966 and of 400,000 by 1975, or roughly twice the earlier estimates. A rapidly growing city of this size would present social problems of major dimensions. Aware of this, the planners had already instituted several studies of the human side of the equation.

One study, conducted by a social anthropologist, collected basic information about the composition of the population moving into the city, their ways of life and their responses to the changes going on around them. Another social project set up a pilot program to help the in-migrants build their own housing. Other investigations looked into the questions of health, nutrition and family-spending patterns. Still others surveyed migration characteristics, the attitudes of the people toward authority and change and the relative importance they attached to various public services and physical improvements. One of these inquiries, made for the first time in such a situation, was a survey of how people of different backgrounds perceived and rated the importance of particular features of the physical environment.

These investigations proved helpful in several ways. They indicated the need for communication and full explanation of the development program to the people of the community; they highlighted apparent conflicts between the immediate concerns of the residents and the long-range aims of the planners; they pointed up the importance of community participation in planning decisions; above all they sensitized the planning staff to the extraordinary problems and needs of the lowest-income group in the population. For this group it was necessary to work out stable family patterns, to find jobs and housing sites and to develop skills and educational opportunities.

While these studies were being run, plans were made for the

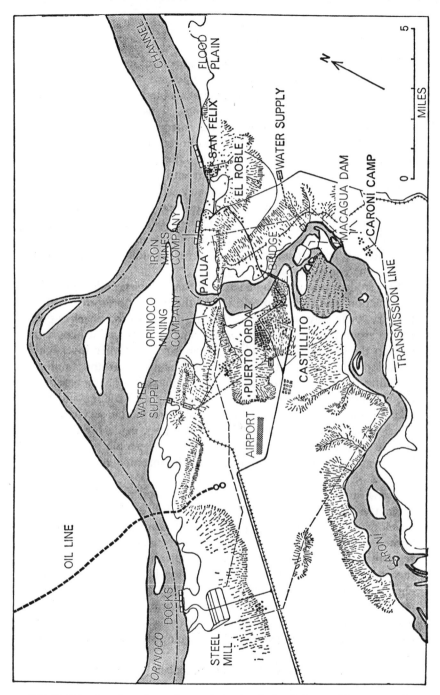

SITE OF CITY stretches along the south bank of the Orinoco. The scattered existing communities include the old town of San Félix (right), mining-company towns and squatters' settlements. Facilities include a steel mill, docks and the new Caroní bridge.

layout of the city. These had to be versatile enough to ensure the orderly future integration of the scattered settlements and at the same time guide decisions on meeting the immediate needs of the citizens. The primary objective was to create conditions that would foster economic growth. While holding to this main aim, the planners also wished to minimize investment expense, recapture the increments in value resulting from the massive investments of the government, make economical, accessible and flexible arrangements suited to different stages of the city's growth, maintain a high standard of design that would serve as a model for developments elsewhere and attract enterprising organizations to Guayana, provide variety and interest in the community's living and social facilities and take advantage of the normal forces of the market rather than run counter to them.

After much discussion it was decided that first consideration had to be given to housing, education and the establishments required by the local government. The location of these facilities had to be related, of course, to the principal industrial and business activities of the city. Here four main considerations were involved: (1) the site was large; (2) the location of the steel plant at the western end made that area the principal center for industrial development; (3) a large proportion of the population, on the other hand, was already living on the eastern side of the site; (4) the most beautiful part of the site was in between, toward the south along the Caroní River. Should the new city be built around the steel plant? The planners finally decided that for several reasons it would be far preferable to form the city by uniting the existing elements. This not only would be less expensive but also would conform to existing growth patterns, would provide greater flexibility and security if the projections proved optimistic, and would encounter less political opposition.

The spread-out character of the city affected the location of various centers and presented difficult transportation issues. It was imperative to reduce the cost and time of travel to the central business district, the civic center and other areas frequented by most of the population. Because a rapid-transit system would prove too expensive an investment for the postulated size of the city and the travel distances, most of the travel would be by automobile: private cars, buses, taxis and *por puestos* (jitneys). With the help of a high-speed computer the staff tested a number of possible arrangements. The alternatives included various combinations of possible locations for jobs, homes and other centers and the different modes of transportation.

For the layout of the city that was selected as optimal from various points of view it turned out that when the city's population reached 250,000, its people would be spending about 12 to 16 percent of their disposable income on transportation in the city. This figure is not far from those in comparable cities in the U.S.: in Los Angeles the average cost is 16 percent, in Cleveland 14 percent, in Chicago 13 percent. Because incomes in Venezuela are considerably lower than in the U.S., however, the travel cost will be a greater burden to the residents of Ciudad Guayana. This burden is inherent in the present low-density settlements and the considerable distance between the industrial center in the west and the main residential areas in the east. In addition, the facilities will not be used efficiently because of the tidal traffic flows. In view of the constraints there was probably no feasible or less expensive alternative. As the residential areas grow westward toward the industrial center in the future, however, the journey to work and the cost should decline.

When it came to planning the location of industry in Ciudad Guayana, the western part of the site was found to be clearly the best area. The steel plant was already there; there is plenty of suitable land around it for building a large complex of heavy industry; the site is usually downwind from the rest of the city, so that its smoke and odors will be blown away from the residential sections. It also has good access to land and water transportation, and truck traffic generated by the industries can reach domestic markets without passing through the city.

The plan developed for this industrial center contemplates ore-reduction plants, foundries and forges as satellites for the steel plant, and also chemical industries, an aluminum plant, building-materials industries, factories for the manufacture of heavy machinery and a reserve area that will be used for truck farming until other new industries come in. Moreover, the planners made provision for light industries, to be located elsewhere in the city. An area east of the heavy-industry center is reserved for the manufacture of consumer goods, a storage and truck-transportation center and commercial facilities around the city's airport. Two other areas destined for light industry are on the eastern side of the Caroní River, close to the old residential settlements.

For the main commercial center, where the principal business offices and retail establishments will be located, the site selected is an area called Alta Vista. Eventually this area will have maximum accessibility from all parts of the city. Alta Vista stands on a height commanding wide views of the city; its terrain is level and allows for inexpensive expansion of the business area, and it is bordered on three sides by still undeveloped land that is admirably suited for residential development. There is every likelihood that before long the Alta Vista business center will become an important revenue producer for the city, helping to finance the heavy investment that must be made in the community. To ensure more rapid development in the early stages, however, the planners decided to detach the civic center from the cultural center, with which it had been combined, and to locate it instead at the eastern end of the Alta Vista plateau. This decision was also justified on the grounds that there are important functional ties between government offices, the courts and the principal business services and establishments. Moreover, at this location the civic center would be visible from a great distance in all directions as a symbol of civic activity.

No less important for the future of the city, in the planners' view, was the building of an attractive cultural center. This is particularly crucial in a new city as an inducement to bring in the enterprising managers, professionals, educators and other specialists of all sorts on whom the creation of a vital community depends so heavily. An excellent site for such a center was available. It is an area, called Punta Vista, at an elbow of the Caroní River near its confluence with the Orinoco. Overlooking the Caroní falls, the site is one of varied terrain and great natural beauty. Within this area space has been assigned for an educational center that will eventually include a technical college, a research establishment, a hotel, clubs, a library, a museum and other institutions. Around the falls there are to be a large public park, which will contain a boat basin and landing, a botanical garden, a zoological garden, an aviary and a variety of other facilities. There is room also for an attractive residential settlement to be built next to the park.

Finally, rounding out the list of specialized areas, a medical center is planned at a site on the eastern side of the Caroní near the San Félix settlement. It will include a major hospital, clinics and allied health services.

Up to this point the plan for Ciudad Guayana consisted of a set of separate centers devoted to specialized land uses. The problem now was to tie them all together—in particular, to join up the largest existing settlement, San Félix, with the planned new city centers. The element in the plan designed to accomplish this was a major highway running from the steel plant at the western end to San Félix in the east. Passing through or close to the other centers along its route, this highway, Avenida Guayana, will link together all the main elements of the city: the area of heavy industry, the airport, the centers of light industry and warehouses, the commercial and civic center, the cultural center, the residential areas, the medical center and the established San Félix community. It will serve as an artery and a backbone, making the city a unified organism.

The highway provides a special opportunity to give the city character and physical distinction. Starting as a heavy-duty road in the industrial area, it will change into a boulevard as it passes through the business and civic center; then it will sweep down the hill into the cultural center, proceed across the Caroní bridge and, as a limited-access highway, go on past residential areas and the medical center and finally enter San Félix as a boulevard. To a driver along the highway the trip will present a succession of different experiences composed of the city's natural sights and varied activities. Probably no other physical element will show the city's features as effectively as this highway, and the planners have given special attention to the avenue's physical and visual aspects. In the design of the road they are considering aesthetics as well as efficiency in the location of the activities it will pass, the handling of road alignments, grades and lighting, the landscaping, the visual impressions and behavior of the people now in Ciudad Guayana.

Unfortunately shortages of staff have precluded the detailed evaluations and revisions that ought to accompany such efforts. Another major problem faced by the designers has been how to provide for a pattern of land uses now while simultaneously planning for new uses that will be possible and appropriate in the future. Partly for this reason the staff is attempting to develop criteria and methods for handling "high" and "low" control zones. This would allow concentration on visually and functionally significant areas. Design competitions, the awarding of prizes for well-designed areas, the setting up of architectural review committees and other positive incentives may be employed. In addition, flexible land-use controls may be established, ranging from general zoning and building regulations to more specific restrictions for key points in the city. In spite of these efforts the odds are that the final results will be far different from the original intent. This is understood by the designers, although they hope that the process will not get out of hand.

The Corporación Venezolana de Guayana was charged with the responsibility not only of planning the city but also of seeing that it was built. First the general plans had to be translated into specific projects, each with a financial budget and a definite time schedule. In addition to housing, for which there was an immediate need, there were three projects that obviously required high priority. One was the main highway, needed not only to establish communication between the developing centers of the city but also to encourage the start of new enterprises, particularly in the commercial areas. Another pressing project was the provision of space and facilities for industry. The third, which soon had to be given temporary precedence over the second, was the development of the commercial center. The strategy decided on there was to bring in large department stores and supermarkets, and to build the headquarters offices of the corporation itself, so that these nuclear establishments would generate other substantial, high-level developments in the area. The original program of building the commercial facilities by 1967 proved to be too leisurely; when it began to look as if key firms would not wait that long but would seek locations elsewhere in the city, the program for the business center was speeded up.

Housing became the thorniest of all the problems. The corporation did not want to get into the housing business; for reasons of protocol and because of its own heavy obligations in many areas it sought to avoid any tasks that might be handled more effectively by other agencies. The Venezuelan government has a special agency, Banco Obrero, for building low-income housing. As time went on, however, it became increasingly clear that Banco Obrero could not meet more than a small fraction of the need in Ciudad Guayana. Nor could the job be done in time by any other organization. The corporation therefore had to resort to a variety of stratagems to get housing built.

To provide mortagage funds the corporation started a savings and loan association. It also made arrangements with a nonprofit organization, the Foundation for Popular Housing, to build 854 houses for middle-income families. The corporation, in collaboration with the Agency for International Development, also offered special guarantees to the International Housing Associates, a private building organization, to induce it to build 800 housing units with less expensive foreign capital; unfortunately it took two years to negotiate the final agreement and clear it through the various government agencies. In addition the corporation has made land available to private builders at reduced prices, adjusted to the income levels of the people for whom the houses are to be built, and has discussed and is still negotiating various other possible arrangements with builders and industrialists. Notwithstanding all these efforts, the corporation has found it necessary to build some houses itself, because it had made an agreement with the steelworkers' union to provide a certain number of houses at stipulated price levels by the end of 1965.

In the experimental project of helping low-income families to build their own homes the corporation provided land, public utilities, schools, loans for construction materials and technical assistance. Interestingly it has turned out that the most important factor in inducing these families to build houses to replace their shanties is the construction of streets; so far the existence of streets has proved a greater inducement than water, sewage facilities, electricity or schools, apparently because it distinguishes city living from country living.

The corporation has established a Municipal Housing Institute in Ciudad Guayana. It will supervise the self-help house-building programs and will mount an independent low-income housing program with funds provided by various sources. The corporation is also studying the use of local building materials and may look into the possibility of financing a plant to produce basic elements for prefabricated houses.

The Corporación Venezolana de Guayana has found it necessary to take an active part in many other phases of the area's physical, economic and social development. In addition to managing and planning the expansion of the steelworks (through a subsidiary), it is building a new dam upstream at Guri, the first stage of which will be completed in 1967 and which will add a capacity of 525,000 kilowatts to the 350,000 kilowatts already available from the present Macagua Dam. The corporation is promoting efforts to attract business enterprises to the city, providing inexpensive sites, conducting preliminary feasibility studies, helping on occasion to obtain investment capital, tax benefits, customs exemptions, leaseback arrangements for plant and equipment and even in some cases equity capital. It is assisting the Venezuelan Ministry of Education to set up facilities to train a skilled labor force for the new industries and high-level educational facilities for professional personnel. It is helping the city government to draft a code of ordinances and to train administrators. Over the next 15 years some $400 million is to be invested in the city's structure of public services, which is expected to engage nearly 10,000 persons.

A circumstance that calls for special comment is that most of the land on which Ciudad Guayana is being developed is publicly owned—a most unusual situation. To begin with, the corporation had acquired nearly all the land in the area of the future city proper, except for the properties of the Orinoco Mining Company and some small private holdings in the vicinity of the company's settlement. Altogether it owned about 40 percent of the land in the Caroní district as a whole. The planners figuratively rubbed their hands with pleasure at the advantages this offered. The corporation appeared able to shape and control the use of the land for a considerable period into the future: it could reserve lands needed for public purposes, and it could capture for its financing needs a reasonable share of the gains from rising land values as the city developed. The latter benefit is important because in Venezuela, as in most developing countries, local communities do not levy taxes of any consequence on real estate.

These advantages did indeed prove to be useful, but they also had some drawbacks. The job of managing the publicly owned land presented a heavy burden to the corporation, which had its hands full with a host of other problems. The private enterprises coming into the city needed outright ownership of their sites to use the land as mortgage security for financing improvements. Moreover, the corporation realized that the image of Ciudad Guayana as a government-owned city might discourage private investment in the building of housing, commercial enterprises and industries.

The corporation decided on a flexible policy. The preponderance of the commercial land and the highly desirable residential and industrial land, which was likely to be most profitable, would be held by the corporation and made available to the users under leases. Other land, including some commercial sites, would be sold, subject to restrictions on the use of the land and perhaps even on the transfer of title until the completion of the developments. In general, land would be sold only when it was necessary to speed up development, and the corporation would try to ensure itself a share of the gains in land value by being a partner in the enterprises or by withholding strategically located parcels from sale.

Ciudad Guayana is now a lusty, booming town whose future is still in the balance. Certainly as it grows it will modify the script written by its planners. All in all it is a unique situation: a new city planted by a tour de force in an isolated frontier region by a comparatively wealthy government (thanks to its oil riches) that has donated the land for the enterprise and called in expert assistance from universities in an advanced country. For all its uniqueness, however, the Ciudad Guayana project has some useful lessons to offer on the strategy of urban planning in developing countries.

The Ciudad Guayana enterprise has demonstrated, first of all, the importance of popular and political support for any such project. By remarkable acumen and leadership the Corporación Venezolana de Guayana managed to maintain an impressive reputation and political backing even during the beginning years when there was little to show for the heavy investment and effort. The project itself brought many problems into sharp relief. For example, we do not yet know how to build simple, expandable and genuinely inexpensive housing quickly, and we still must rely on clumsy, primitive techniques for the analysis and control of land use. The research thus far undertaken on these and similar matters is woefully inadequate. The persistent shortages of staff also made it clear that one of the hardest tasks is to determine not only what must be done but also what problems the policy-maker must live with, given the constraints and opportunities. For the same reason it has proved even more difficult to innovate than appeared possible at first. Experiments must be few and critical and adequate means must be devised for getting feedback from them. On the other hand, the university connections established by the corporation make it likely that several significant studies will emerge describing what was done.

The unusual collaboration between the Venezuelan corporation and the Joint Center for Urban Studies of M.I.T. and Harvard has itself been an instructive experience. In the approach to the problems of Ciudad Guayana there were not only individual variations in point of view but also more deep-rooted differences in outlook between the Venezuelan experts and their foreign consultants from the U.S. Inescapably, conflicts arose in the course of the work. Such conflicts involve more than personalities. Groups of human beings working together develop styles of acting and valuing and conceptions of reality that suit the situations they confront, and these situations vary. The foreign technical expert not only has a different native language and different past experience but also is subject to the pulls of a career line different from that of his resident counterpart. They have different professional audiences and different personal futures to build. There are no simple rules on how to deal with this problem beyond emphasis on the obvious: In the choice of staff, ability and common objectives are necessary, not sufficient, conditions; sincere respect for different views and sympathy for failings are also essential qualities.

One of the general benefits that may emerge from the Ciudad Guayana project is the demonstration that the political leaders and builders of cities can profit from formal enlistment of the skills and resources of knowledge available in universities. The universities too have gained much from this adventure in realism. Perhaps the outstanding lesson of the Venezuelan experience will be a demonstration of the value of creating appropriate mechanisms with which to assess and link the growth potentials of the city and region with the national goals for development. Economic, social and physical plans—jointly prepared within this framework—help to ensure consistency, to guide the policy-maker in the process of making critical decisions and to promote more effective urban, regional and national development.

New York:
A Metropolitan Region

· BENJAMIN CHINITZ

Within the region of which New York is the central city are 550 separate municipal governments. How can the sometimes mutual and sometimes conflicting interests of these communities be unified?

IN THE U.S., as in other countries that were early participants in the industrial revolution, large-scale urbanization began in the latter half of the 19th century. There was a steady migration from rural to urban places—from the countryside to towns and cities across the nation. In the past few decades the process has taken a somewhat different turn: the number of urban places is still increasing, but most of the growth in population is occurring in existing and indeed long-established urban areas. And although urban places all over the country are participating in this growth, it is occurring predominantly in large clusters of urban places that have come to be known as metropolitan areas. It is there that the "scale" of urban living—in sheer numbers of people and extent of development—is largest and is steadily becoming larger.

Exactly how is a metropolitan area defined? The Bureau of the Census designates as a "standard metropolitan statistical area" any

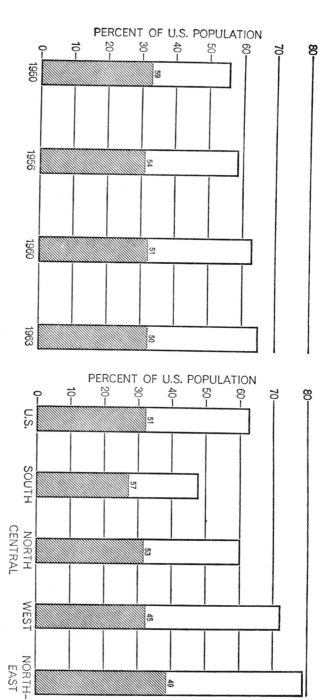

PERCENT OF U.S. POPULATION

1950 — 59

1956 — 54

1960 — 51

1963 — 50

PERCENT OF U.S. POPULATION living in metropolitan areas is rising as the areas grow and as people move in. The central cities' proportion of the metropolitan population is decreasing (shaded portion).

PERCENT OF U.S. POPULATION

U.S. — 51

SOUTH — 57

NORTH CENTRAL — 53

WEST — 45

NORTH-EAST — 49

NORTHEAST is the census region in which the largest percentage of the population is concentrated in metropolitan areas. Central-city share of the metropolitan population is smallest in the West.

county with a central city of 50,000 or more inhabitants, together
with contiguous counties that meet certain standards of urbanism
and connection to the center. In 1940 there were 140 metropolitan
areas containing 48 percent of the U.S. population; in 1963 there
were 216 such areas containing 65 percent of the population. The
growth of the metropolitan areas is mainly the growth of their
suburbs; in recent years the population of the largest central cities
has actually declined. Suburbs that were once strung out along
radial railroad lines have filled in as the automobile erased the old
advantage of "a short walk from the station." Nearby cities have
been adsorbed to the center.

Still, the suburbs and the smaller cities retain their own governments, their own schools and sewer systems, zoning ordinances
and garbage trucks. A metropolitan area tends to be integrated
economically; its communities have fundamental problems in
common; its residents commute, shop, visit and telephone across
boundaries. The metropolitan areas nonetheless remain political
jungles with thickets of competing governments. Since there can
be no doubt that an increasingly larger share of the country's
population will be living and working in metropolitan areas, it is
important to learn how these areas can organize their affairs
rationally in spite of the diverse self-interests of competing political jurisdictions.

Many of the largest metropolitan areas in the country are in the
Northeast, where they form the great belt of high-density development that stretches almost without interruption for 400 miles
along the East Coast from Boston to Washington. In overall size
and density this collection of metropolises is unique in the world,
so much so that the geographer Jean Gottmann invented the
term "megalopolis" to distinguish it from ordinary metropolitan
clusters. At the center of the megalopolis, stretching almost 100
miles from southwest to northeast, is the New York area.

The New York metropolitan area is arbitrarily limited by the
Census Bureau's definition to nine counties with a 1960 population
of 10,700,000. A more meaningful unit is the New York–Northeastern New Jersey Consolidated Area (population 14,700,000).
Still more comprehensive is the New York Metropolitan Region,
which embraces the whole economic and social complex centered
on Manhattan Island. The New York Region was defined many

INCREASE OF REGION'S POPULATION since 1860 and as projected by the Regional Plan Association to 1985 is broken down into curves for Manhattan, the core and the three surrounding rings. The population of Manhattan and the core is actually decreasing.

years ago by the Regional Plan Association and has been analyzed exhaustively in the New York Metropolitan Region Study it sponsored five years ago. The Region's limits are set partly by the commuting "watershed" and partly by the extent to which the outlying areas are influenced by the center, look to the center and, as the Regional Plan Association puts it, would have a different character than they do if they were moved 50 miles farther from the city. This New York Region covers 6,900 square miles of 22 counties in the states of New York, New Jersey and Connecticut, and as of 1960 it had 16,139,000 residents.

Although California has overtaken New York as the most populous state, it will be some time before the Los Angeles metropolitan area, in spite of its huge size, exceeds the New York Region in population. The density of the New York area is not likely ever to be duplicated in the U.S. This density ranges from 77,000 people per square mile in Manhattan and about 25,000 per square mile in New York City as a whole to about 200 per square mile at the edges of the Region; the overall density of the Region is 2,337 per square mile and the density of even the part outside New York City is 1,265 per square mile. In terms of density and degree of development the Regional Plan Association subdivides the Region into a core and inner, intermediate and outer rings.

In a nation of metropolises, New York is unique. With 9 percent of the country's population, the Region provides some 40 percent of all U.S. jobs in national-market wholesaling activities, more than a third of the jobs in finance, almost a quarter of the business and professional service jobs and, somewhat surprisingly, almost 12 percent of the jobs in manufacturing. The Region is remarkably center-oriented. Half of its jobs are within five miles of Times Square in Manhattan; most of the activities in which the Region is nationally dominant are concentrated in the Manhattan business district: finance, radio and television, advertising, publishing, fashion and corporate headquarters. Every day more than three million people come to work in that part of Manhattan south of 61st Street.

Employment figures are a significant measure of New York's national role, but obviously they leave much unsaid. The city fulfills for the U.S. many of the highest functions of a metropolis. The clichés are true: the height and breadth of the city are overwhelming; the nervous energy of its people, the variety of their origins and attitudes and goals are stimulating; its output of ideas, books, articles, paintings, plays and music, of fads and styles, of protest and restless dissatisfaction influences the entire country and the world. For years the city has pioneered in social advances and the use of government to humanize an industrial society, and in spite of profound difficulties its government is remarkable for the range of its services and the expertise of its personnel.

New York City's budget is second only to that of the Federal Government, and it accounts for more than half of the Region's public expenditures. Beyond the city limits the counties, towns, boroughs, cities, villages and hundreds of school districts, fire districts and sewer districts provide government services and regulate various aspects of the residents' lives. In all there are 550 municipal governments and another 900 or so special districts. Superimposed on all of these are the three state governments and a number of special-purpose regional agencies. Fifty years ago, as Robert C. Wood of the Massachusetts Institute of Technology pointed out in a volume of the Metropolitan Region Study, the multiplicity of local governments would not have been a crucial factor in an examination of how the Region functions socially and economically; today it is, because "the Service State has settled in."

If New York is in many respects unique, it is nevertheless the archetypical metropolitan region. What are the significant aspects and dimensions of urban scale in a place such as New York that make the metropolitan region a qualitative as well as a quantitative frontier? Whatever problems may be associated with the accommodation of urban living, do they simply increase in proportion to scale or are they exaggerated—or possibly minimized—by scale? Or do they change their character altogether? Do we require wholly new institutional mechanisms and policies as the scale of urbanization increases, or simply more of the same?

What is peculiarly urban and a function of urban scale is the interdependence of the various urban spaces and its corollary: specialized uses of urban space. An isolated community needs to provide within its own borders for the space needs of its households and industries—areas for housing, for recreation, for shops, for factories, for transportation terminals, for public buildings. By engaging in trade with other communities the isolated community can of course avoid certain kinds of space commitment altogether: cities do not need to set aside land for agriculture. To a certain extent the residents of an isolated community will travel to other communities to meet some of their needs. Nonetheless, on the whole the balance in the uses of space in such communities is struck at the level of the individual community, and the scope for specialized uses of space is necessarily quite restricted.

As transportation becomes faster and more convenient, however, and as the community grows in size and wealth, the opportunities for specialization in the uses of space are enhanced. Now one large modern school, centrally located, can take the place of many small schools scattered about the countryside. The regional shopping center can displace dozens of neighborhood stores. The bigger and better park with a beach can serve a wider radius. The better industrial sites 10 miles away can now be used exclusively for that purpose, and adequate space for residential development can be provided elsewhere within reasonable commuting distance.

Urbanization, metropolitanization and megalopolitanization are serial stages in the broadening of opportunities for the specialized uses of land. The specialization, however, comes about in real life not according to some rational plan but in response to geography, economics, politics and accidents of history. In the New York Region one sees not only variety and specialization but also what Wood calls the "segregation of resources and needs."

In general, the older and more densely populated cities of the Region have the needs and the outlying areas have the resources. New York City's government expenditures amounted to 10.3 percent of its total personal income in 1955; in the other New York counties the figure was 9.3 percent and in the New Jersey part of the Region it was only 6.4. Although New York City and its jobs are the source of much suburban wealth, and although the city must help to transport commuters, protect them and provide services for the offices and stores and factories where they work, the commuters pay no taxes directly to New York City. The core area and some of the older inner-ring cities such as Elizabeth in Union County or Mount Vernon in Westchester County face rising expenditures to cope with social problems, but it is the newer suburbs that obtain new revenue from middle- and high-income residents, new industries and offices. Inner cities need industry, but industry is pulled outward to hamlets along the superhighways.

Even in newly developing areas in the Region's intermediate and outer rings the opportunity for specialization brings with it the increasing risk of inconsistent patterns of land use when the facts of interdependence are ignored. The heart of the urban problem is therefore the unleashing of the new-found freedom of choice in the allocation of land for various uses and the reconciliation of heretofore independent choices. The larger the scale and intensity of urbanization, the greater the opportunity for gain and the risk of loss. The difficulty and risk are increased in a metropolitan area by the multiplicity of jurisdictions. If it is hard for an individual community to allocate uses for open land, to enforce zoning, to anticipate school or recreation or highway needs, it is much more difficult for 550 sovereign municipalities to do so. For a number of reasons, then, the New York Region is pioneering in establishing the scope of the metropolitan problem. Is it also pioneering in developing the proper responses to the challenge?

Before one can even attempt such an appraisal there are a number of basic issues to consider that complicate any discussion of "proper" metropolitan responses. In the first place, one cannot equate what is best for a society as a whole with what is best for each segment of it. Free trade is better for the world than tariff barriers and other kinds of restriction, but a given country may sometimes be better off if it imposes restrictions. Similarly, if it is true that, as the scale of the urban area increases, a reorientation of the spatial pattern will produce economic benefits, it does not follow that each community stands to gain from the shake-up; even for some that would gain in the long run the transition could be quite painful. The role a new order might assign to a particular community might be far less appealing to its residents than the role it now plays. Furthermore, as long as the community is left with the responsibility of striking a balance between revenue and expenditure, it cannot afford to take a passive role in the determination of these magnitudes. The new order could well assign to the community a mixture of land uses that would generate expenditures in excess of the revenues that could reasonably be expected from taxation of these uses. Such an outcome might seem appropriate from the regional point of view but would be quite intolerable from the point of view of the individual community.

The logic of the situation, in the opinion of some observers, leads inevitably to the conclusion that the new order requires the total dissolution of the old: the elimination of local community autonomy and the establishment of metropolitan or even regional government. The argument is that only at these higher levels can politics and economics be made mutually consistent.

This resolution of the dilemma, as appealing as it may be, is not one that can be counted on to solve the problems of metropolitan regions. A community that waits for a whole new order to displace the old, and does not confront the challenge of reconciling the new with the old, runs a serious risk of waiting in vain. Beyond that, one can legitimately quarrel with the principle as well as the realism of the argument for metropolitan government. It implies that, whereas the town or the county was once the logical political unit from an economic point of view, the metropolitan area is now in that favored position. This is altogether too simple a view of the dynamics of urban development. For some functions the municipality retains a distinct advantage as a political unit, for others the county is advantageous and for still others the metropolitan area is—and so on up the line. The process has not come to an end; what will the advocates of metropolitan government say when—perhaps soon—"megalopolitan" government is proposed?

I do not mean to suggest, at the other extreme, that a region must accept its political heritage without change. Innovation comes, however, through adapting the old as well as adding the new. It is in this light that one must appraise the progress made in accommodating the new economic order in urban areas.

A second complicating issue, not unrelated to the first, is the matter of specifying the new order. The advocates of metropolitan government imply at times that were it not for the politics that keep confusing things one could map a clear path to the ideal solution because it is unique and can be discovered by technical analysis. This fallacy betrays a common misunderstanding of the very nature of technological progress and economic change. The essence of any new order is the extension of the range of the possible. Because men can go to the moon, however, it does not follow that men must go to the moon. It is only by surveying technical possibilities in the light of community values and preferences that one can arrive at a unique response to new opportunities. To take a metropolitan view does not obviate the necessity for articulating community preferences.

Why can the matter of preference not be left to the marketplace? After all, the larger part of the spatial realignment of the metropolis will occur through the cumulative decisions of households in their choice of residential locations and of business units in their choice of industrial and commercial locations. They will see the new opportunities and their preferences will be manifested in the locations they choose in the light of these new opportunities.

There is no doubt that private decisions do ultimately reshape the metropolis, but public decisions set the bounds that shape these decisions. The public built the Verrazano-Narrows Bridge from Brooklyn to Staten Island (Richmond) that has suddenly opened the last rural part of New York City to massive residential development by private persons. (The public neglected to regulate the planless, headlong rush to subdivide, to bulldoze and to build badly designed houses that are currently scarring the Staten Island landscape.)

The public did not invent the internal-combustion engine or develop the conveyor belt, but it does build highways and bridges and it does establish the zoning regulations that permit one-story factory construction in some locations and prohibit it in others, thereby influencing the use of conveyor belts. The public translates technical progress into opportunities with permits and price tags attached to them. Governments maintain order, regulate and provide services. Moreover, the public sector, like the private, has increasing freedom in the choice of locations for public facilities. Parks, water-supply and garbage-disposal systems, schools, government buildings, libraries—all these ingredients of a location strategy are entirely in the public domain. This domain is getting larger every day.

In summary, the appraisal of the response to the challenge of large-scale urbanization takes these propositions for granted: that the new order will not be implemented efficiently by private choice, that it cannot be implemented by the substitution of one giant local government where many existed before, and that a way must yet be found to inject a large measure of regional planning and decision-making.

A regional approach is more likely to filter down from the top than to work its way up from the bottom. This fact of life is particularly evident in three fields in which "regional enterprises" must inevitably play major roles: transportation, water supply and urban development.

There is disagreement about the extent to which the megalopolis has become a meaningful intermetropolitan "region," but there can be no doubt that the communities from Boston to Washington do interact with regard to travel along their major axis: the so-called Northeast Corridor. Traffic along the Corridor continues to build up every year. It is being accommodated by miles of new superhighways and by large increases in airport facilities and air service. The railroads, on the other hand, have not found it profitable or even possible to spend the money required to improve their service. As Corridor traffic doubles in the next 20 years or so, the tendency will be to accommodate it with still more highways and more, bigger and faster airplanes. This may well not be a desirable solution. Perhaps enough of the Northeast has been paved; perhaps airports are already inconveniently far from cities. Is there any way to shape the future instead of letting it creep up on us? Only the Federal Government has been able to set in motion an effort to take a comprehensive look at the problem and come up with proposed solutions. Through its Northeast Corridor Project the Department of Commerce is studying the economic and technical aspects of mass transportation on the ground, working toward short-term improvement of train service while it considers more advanced forms of surface travel at speeds approaching those of airplane schedules.

The Corridor program is unusual; most Federal intervention in transportation planning has ignored the railroads in favor of the truck, the automobile and the bus—and of course the airplane. The Federal Aviation Agency promotes air travel and airport construction. Through its Bureau of Public Roads and the state highway departments, the Federal Government has financed highway development in the New York Region, especially as part of its national Interstate Highway program. Although these arteries are planned primarily as elements of a national network, they create significant improvements in access within the Region. A specific route may often offend local sensibilities, but since roads have to lead somewhere, communities are generally more willing to accept decisions of higher jurisdictions in highway matters than in other endeavors.

Within the Region the agencies that have played the most important role in fashioning the transport network are the Port of New York Authority and the Triborough Bridge and Tunnel Authority. It is hardly possible to take a trip of any length by automobile without moving over a facility constructed by one of these agencies. The Triborough Authority operates strictly within New York City but the Port of New York Authority is the creature of a compact between the states of New York and New Jersey and operates over much of the Region, specializing in spanning the Hudson River and in building and operating the Region's airports.

The Federal Government, the state governments and the special authorities, then, bear the major responsibility of caring for the New York Region's transportation needs. These are giant organizations with impressive financial resources that do not fluctuate with the vagaries of local public finance that plague municipal and county governments. They derive their revenue mainly from user charges: gasoline taxes and tolls. They can presumably see above the confusion of local rivalries and plan for the future in comprehensive terms.

The view from the top has limitations, however, and is considerably less comprehensive than one might expect. The government highway agencies and the public authorities are devoted to the service of the automobile. There has been no agency at the top charged with the job of coordinating all transportation activities in the Region, rail as well as highway.

There was an attempt to establish such an agency in the 1950's. The Metropolitan Rapid Transit Commission was set up by New York and New Jersey to study overall needs and attempt to reconcile rail and automobile transportation. It began by failing to get necessary financial support from the states or the railroads, turned to the Port Authority for help and thereby biased its efforts in favor of preserving autonomous highway building activities on a pay-their-own-way basis. In 1958 the M.R.T.C. came up with proposals for tying New Jersey's railroads into the New York City subway system, to be financed by new county property taxes. There was immediate opposition from New York

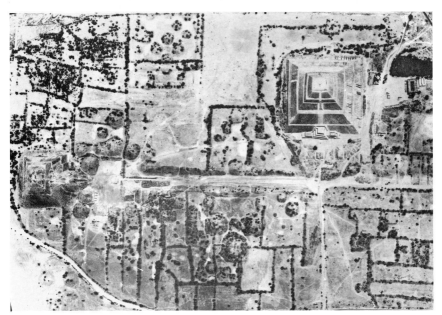

TEOTIHUACAN is an extensive urban site near modern Mexico City that flourished during the first millennium A.D. The full extent of the city is not yet known, but it continues for miles beyond the area shown. Aerial and ground surveys show that the north-south axis of the city was formed by a broad avenue (the Street of the Dead) that starts at the Pyramid of the Moon (far left) and runs past the larger Pyramid of the Sun (upper right). The east-west axis of Teotihuacán was formed by similar avenues. Although primarily a market and religious center for the surrounding countryside, Teotihuacán probably contained a resident population of 100,000 or more within its 16 square miles.

A ROMAN RESORT in Italy, Pompeii was buried by 18 feet of ash from Vesuvius in A.D. 79 after a lifetime of at least 400 years. Its rectangular ground plan was presumably designed by the Etruscans, who were among the city's first residents in pre-Roman days. Population estimates for the resort city are uncertain; its amphitheater (far left), however, could seat 20,000 people. Forgotten soon after its burial, Pompeii was rediscovered in 1748.

A RENAISSANCE CITY, Lucca in northern Italy is no longer contained within the bastioned circuit of its walls, which were begun in 1504 and completed in 1645. Lucca's seesaw history is like that of many other southern European cities. A Roman town during the Punic wars, it was the site of Caesar's triumvirate meeting with Pompey and Crassus in 60 B.C. and was pillaged by Odoacer at the fall of the Roman Empire in A.D. 476. A fortress city once again by the seventh century A.D., Lucca had become a prosperous manufacturing center, specializing in the weaving of silk textiles, by the 12th century. It continues to produce silk and other textiles today.

TOKYO is viewed from an altitude of two miles in this photograph. Area shown is a portion of Ikebukuro, a commercial and residential district in the northwestern part of the city. The broad gray lane traversing the photograph from left center at top to left center at bottom is part of the Yamate rail line, which rings central Tokyo. Along the rail line near the top are the buildings of a government-sponsored housing development. To the left of the rail line near the center is the Gukushuin educational complex.

RENEWAL AREA in downtown Stockholm includes and surrounds the five tall buildings near the center of the photograph. The project was planned as the new business center of the city. Area at bottom left, where construction is under way, will be the site of a complex of fountains and underground restaurants constructed in the shape of concentric "superellipses." To left of the tall buildings is a shopping mall exclusively for pedestrians.

SUBURB OF TÄBY is under development seven miles north of Stockholm. The arc-shaped buildings contain 1,548 apartments; the eight 15-story buildings, a total of 1,180 apartments. In keeping with plans for suburbs, Täby has spacious parking lots, a shopping center (left center), and ready access to a suburban train (left). Oval at the top of the photograph is the new Stockholm race track.

HONG KONG, part of which appears in the aerial photograph on the opposite page, combines features of land use encountered in cities of industrialized areas with features encountered in cities of underdeveloped areas. One such feature in under-developed areas is the pre-emption of land for residential purposes by squatters. On the hillsides at far left center and upper right are squatter shacks. The harbor at lower center is filled with hundreds of squatter sampans. The oblong buildings at upper right are nine-story walk-ups erected by the government to provide one-room apartments.

BEFORE LEVITT & SONS ARRIVED, the region shown in this aerial photograph was Pennsylvania farmland. Land use had changed little in two centuries. The only distinctly modern feature is the oval track of the Langhorne raceway, one mile in circumference.

AFTER LEVITT ARRIVED in 1952 the land was put to new use. Between 1952 and 1958 more than 17,000 homes, most of them priced below $15,000, were built in the new community called Levittown, Pa. Only a small portion of the eight-square-mile development appears in this photograph. If Levittown were a political entity, which it is not, its present population of more than 65,000 would make it the 11th largest city in the state.

PRE-EMPTION OF LAND BY SQUATTERS is vividly apparent in this view of part of Casablanca, the largest city of Morocco. In the foreground is a planned array of new buildings. Beyond them is a large area covered with tiny, sheet-iron-roofed squatter shacks.

CHICAGO SLUM was photographed in 1944 from a building on Federal Street. In the 1950's this neighborhood was demolished and rebuilt under the auspices of the U.S. Urban Renewal Authority, the Chicago Housing Authority, and several other agencies.

RENEWED NEIGHBORHOOD was photographed from same perspective in 1965. Federal Street has been rerouted and is now adjacent to the railroad tracks. The development at center and right consists of eight units housing mostly middle-income families.

City and from New Jersey communities on the ground of expense, from the New York City Transit Authority on the ground of feasibility, even from regional groups on the ground that the plan was not comprehensive enough. The Port Authority rejected alternative proposals that it become an integrated rail and highway agency. The M.R.T.C. plan died, the commuter railroads continued to lose money and close down and the Region's highway network continued to grow. In transportation, regionalism turns out to be incidental to the main mission of the various agencies, which is to forge ahead on projects that will justify themselves in the cash register of the agency while adding to the Region's capacity for accommodating travel.

Of course the construction of highways and river crossings serves precisely to create a diffusion of access and thereby to promote spatial specialization and enhance freedom of locational choice. It was the construction of the Hudson River tunnels and bridges, for example, that made the New Jersey cities on the west bank desirable locations for manufacturers and wholesalers seeking to distribute their goods in New York City. At the same time the river crossings dealt a heavy blow to New Jersey's railroads. Continued improvement of the highway network, including the building of the Verrazano-Narrows Bridge, tends to dilute the New Jersey advantage, transferring it to Long Island. Now the Triborough Authority has proposed a new bridge to connect central Long Island with Westchester County, a move that would keep much Corridor traffic out of New York City but at the same time increase the pull toward outlying areas for manufacturing and distributing firms.

Given the broad ramifications of transportation decisions, there is reason to be uneasy about a decision-making process so limited in its perspective. There is more than the balance of rail and high-. way at stake. As I have pointed out, no precise pattern of land use is dictated by technology; the choice among possible patterns entails taking into account both the impact of land use on transport needs and the feedback impact on land use of transport investments—and all this for the Region as a whole. At this stage the Region simply does not have the regional institutions to plan in this comprehensive way.

If there is progress in this direction, again the pressure is mainly from the top down. The Federal Government has recently stipulated that grants for highway construction in metropolitan areas must be preceded by comprehensive land-use and transportation plans. A new agency, the Tri-State Transportation Committee, has been set up in the New York area with Federal as well as state and New York City representatives and with substantial Federal aid, charged with coordinating transportation and land-use planning in the Region as a whole. In spite of the Federal carrot there has been considerable resistance to the creation of such an agency from one of the participating states (New Jersey), and it is too soon to be confident that the agency will achieve a higher order of effective regional planning than has hitherto been possible.

Like transportation, the provision of water for the metropolis is a regional problem; it is broader than that, in fact, since the Region must reach beyond its borders to find adequate supplies. New York City began in the middle of the 19th century to put together a system of reservoirs and conduits that now reaches far upstate to the headwaters of the Delaware River. The Delaware River runs through New Jersey, Pennsylvania and Delaware; it is the water source for Philadelphia, Camden and many other communities and its use is therefore regulated by an interstate commission. The five-year drought in the Northeast has brought to a head a megalopolitan-scale argument involving four states and a number of major cities. Predictably it is the Federal Government that is now intervening with new study groups and "task forces" and proposals to extend the reservoir system into the Adirondack Mountains.

In recent years a new field of government activity has had increasing impact on the shaping of the Region: housing and urban development. Here the Federal Government is heavily involved, but local action remains critical. (New York City, for example, has been far more aggressive in obtaining Federal funds for public low-cost housing than other cities.) Federal mortgage-insurance programs have not been intended to guide development, but by making homeownership possible for middle-income people they have stimulated the flight to the suburbs, unintentionally vitiating newer Federal activities designed to revive central cities. Urban renewal has been more successful in rehabilitating business districts than in renewing residential areas [see "The Renewal of Cities," by Nathan Glazer, page 175]. The urban renewal program provides funds with which cities and smaller communities are encouraged to plan their land uses comprehensively, but in many cases municipalities have done so without sufficient thought to competing land uses in adjacent communities. The Government is now beginning to place more emphasis on regional planning for renewal projects.

In transportation, water supply and redevelopment regional, state and Federal agencies are involved. In most other fields the local governments are largely in command. How much regional planning has emerged from voluntary cooperation among them? Not much, Wood decided after a thorough study of the question. "Each government is preoccupied with its own problems," he wrote, "and collectively the governments are not prepared to formulate general policies for guiding economic development, nor to make generalized responses to the financial pressures generated by urbanization. They are not in a position to establish and enforce public criteria for appropriate conditions of growth or to provide public services which the private sector requires on a Region-wide basis. By their organization, financing and philosophy they forswear the opportunity for the exercise of these larger powers."

This characterization may seem harsh in the light of the numer-- ous intergovernment arrangements that do exist, some for consultation and some for the provision of services. These arrangements are limited, however, both in the kinds of activity involved and in the extent of territory embraced. Moreover, even where communities are quick to recognize the savings that may be effected through cooperation, they are loath to surrender their sovereignty, and above all their control of the pattern of land use within their borders. The chief executives of the Region's counties and many cities have been associated since 1956 in the Metropolitan Regional Council. The council has served as a forum and has sponsored some joint studies, but it has no clear area of influence and no power—even advisory power. Several years ago an effort to give it a measure of power and some financial support through state legislation was met by fierce suburban opposition. There were cries that the plan was "made in Moscow," that the council would become a "supergovernment," that "Westchester will end up as part of the Bronx." As a result the council is now less effective than ever.

If metropolitan government is not the panacea it is often assumed to be and intergovernment cooperation is hard to come by, what hope is there for regional planning as a vital influence in shaping the patterns of land use within the Region? There are two forces at work that seem to offer some promise.

One is the growing understanding within the Federal Government that in operating from the top down it bears the greatest responsibility for being consistent. The Bureau of Public Roads and the Housing and Home Finance Agency are finally getting better acquainted with each other in the state capitals and city halls. They are jointly financing studies of land use and transportation, and their own staffs as well as their client municipalities and the municipalities' professional consultants are becoming more comprehensive in their outlook. The creation in August 1965 of a Cabinet-level Department of Housing and Urban Development reflects the growing recognition that efforts to cope with metropolitan problems need to be closely coordinated.

A second force is the gradual but persistent growth of nonlocal revenue as a fraction of local resources. Grants-in-aid from Federal and state governments are increasing much faster than revenues from local property taxes. This significant trend strikes at the very heart of the problem of achieving intergovernment cooperation. As long as local governments are compelled to strike a financial balance within their communities, it is hopeless to expect them to surrender their parochial interests in favor of regionalism. To the extent that the tie between local income and local taxable values is broken, therefore, the gates are opened for a more sympathetic response to regional priorities.

In this domain may also lie the opportunity for a really imaginative and basic innovation in intergovernmental relations. The sharing of tax revenues among municipalities now occurs largely as a by-product of the growth of Federal and state programs. A frontal attack on the problem would require municipalities to share with one another part of the revenues that normally accrue to them directly. The basis for all such relations, however, must lie in improved techniques for calculating the costs and benefits to individual communities that arise from their accommodation to any new order and the cost to the region of their continued refusal to make such an accommodation.

The Uses of Land
in Cities

· CHARLES ABRAMS

In cities all over the world land is used for specialized purposes such as housing and industry. One of the main problems of any city is how to control these uses to enable the city to function and evolve.

THE CURRENT URBANIZATION of life all over the world is bringing about a profound change in man's attitude toward land and living room. Up to a generation ago economists and political scientists speculating on the future of the human race were haunted by apprehensions about land shortage and land monopoly. These worries of the classical land economists, from Thomas Malthus to John Stuart Mill, were crystallized in Henry George's demand for a single tax on land to prevent the land monopolists and landlords from becoming the rulers of the earth. Today such notions seem little more than a reminder of a credulous past. In the present industrial economy intangible forms of property—money, stocks, credit—have replaced land as the symbols of wealth and power. Most important, the use of land itself is measured on a new scale.

On the urban scale of *Lebensraum* (say 50 persons, or approximately 12 families, per acre) West Germany alone could house the entire present population of the earth. At this same density the entire population of the U.S. could be accommodated on the West Coast, with nearly everyone having a view of the Pacific. About 70 percent of the U.S. population is now concentrated in urban and suburban communities occupying in total only a little more than 1 percent of the nation's land area, and the greatly increased population expected by the year 2000 will still take up only a little more than 2 percent of the land. In "right little, tight little" England 4 percent of the land is occupied by 40 percent of the people. Even in crowded Japan, which only recently fought a desperate war for space, half an hour's train ride from the center of Tokyo takes one into the open country of paddy fields.

For urban man there is no shortage of land. There are problems of effective use and organization of his space, but essentially the urban system can provide him with plenty of room for work, for sleep, for play and for a manifold range of activities. This is not to say that land for many of mankind's needs, such as producing food, has ceased to be a prime concern, or that urbanization has reduced the need for population control. What it does mean is that the shift from a predominantly rural world to a predominantly urban one is changing a situation of land hunger into one of land abundance. Man's old drive for outward expansion can now be redirected toward *intensive* expansion of the opportunities for work and living within the region where he lives. Thus the rise and growth of the modern city system may reduce a historic cause of war and conquest: the quest for living space.

The intensive development of the city—that is, the proper use of its land—is still an almost uncharted frontier. Urban land economics, it must be admitted, can hardly be called a true discipline as yet. There are few experts, and fewer theories, on the subject. There is, however, a body of established facts and observations with which to start.

The modern metropolis, as has been pointed out elsewhere in this book, is limited to an area with a radius of about an hour's travel time from the center to the outskirts. Within that area, space must be provided for housing, offices, shops, factories, recreation, parks, government buildings, utilities, roads, bridges, parking spaces, railroads, airfields, schools, universities and cemeteries. (In England, which is more pressed for urban space than most countries, authorities are now urging families to cremate their dead to

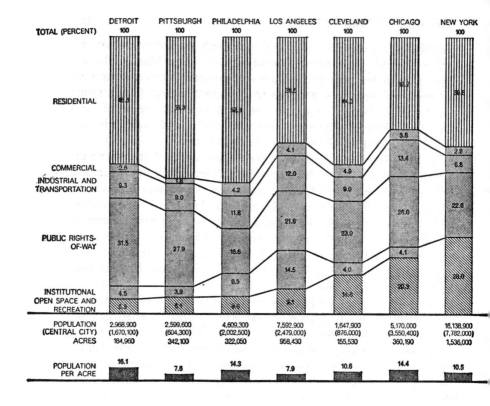

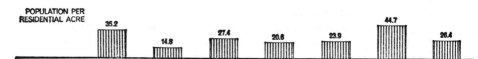

LAND USE IN METROPOLITAN REGIONS shows a wide range of variation. The seven regions are arranged so that percentage of open space increases from left to right. Even though the figure for New York includes land devoted to institutional use, the combined figure is higher than the combined figure that can be obtained for any other region. This suggests that New York indeed has more open space than other regions. The population figures designated by vertical-lined and diagonal-lined bars include surrounding regions in addition to the central city. The population of the central city appears in parentheses. Populations shown are for 1960 except for Chicago (1956) and Detroit (1953). Note the range in population densities. The data for this illustration were assembled by the Regional Plan Association.

forestall the expansion of the cemeteries.) As a city grows, all these demands for space of course increase. Hans Blumenfeld observes, however, that an hour's travel radius takes in a great deal of territory [see "The Modern Metropolis," page 40]. The space problems of metropolises arise not from actual shortages of land but from lack of planning, waste of space, and from the unnecessary despoliation of good environments.

In California, for example, three million acres of the state's attractive landscape are currently being threatened by the steam shovel. In Santa Clara County alone one dairy farm a week has been lost to subdivisions. In England the "rape" of the countryside shocked aesthetic sensibilities and caused the government to impose drastic controls on the location of industries. What these various cases illustrate is that urbanized nations are faced with problems of land allotment and location of activities rather than with land shortage per se.

In the less developed countries the cities have a space problem of a different kind: what to do with the people flooding in from the impoverished rural districts. Armies of squatters are taking over every vacant space, not only on the outskirts but even in the centers of towns, and putting up shacks of tin, wood or cardboard. In the metropolitan areas of Peru, for example, the number of squatters grew from 45,000 in 1940 to 958,000 by 1960. Metropolitan Manila in the Philippines had nearly 283,000 squatters in 1963, and their number is growing so rapidly that it is expected to reach 800,000 by 1980. In Davao squatters have settled down on a parkway running from the city hall to the retail center. In Caracas, the capital of Venezuela, more than 35 percent of the city's total population are squatters; in Maracaibo, 50 percent; in Santiago, Chile, 25 percent; in Ankara, Turkey, nearly 50 percent; in Istanbul, more than 30 percent. So it goes in cities on every continent. Most of the squatter camps have no services: no schools, no sewers, not even water, except what the squatters fetch in pails or oil drums or buy at high cost from peddlers. Garbage piles up around the shacks. The settlements are fire and health hazards, but the city governments are almost helpless to enforce controls or do much to improve their condition.

Compounding the squatter problem in cities of the underdeveloped countries is the problem of land speculation and high land prices. In the metropolises of advanced countries land prices are kept under some control by taxation and modern transport systems that make a wide area accessible. In the U.S., for instance, the land cost (without utilities) represents no more than about a quarter of the total cost of a multiple dwelling in the central area and no more than 10 percent of the cost of a house in the suburbs. In the less developed countries, on the other hand, the land price often amounts to 60 percent of the combined cost of house and lot. Frequently the owners of strategically placed land will not sell it at all, holding it for future sale at swollen prices when the demand soars. Moreover, high land cost is not the only obstacle to home building and ownership in these countries. With the annual family income often less than $100 a year, land at any price is beyond the family's means. The would-be home builder cannot raise money by a mortgage because there is no mortgage system, and to obtain a personal loan he must pay as much as 100 percent per annum in interest. In some countries it is impossible to get a clear title to a site because there is no land-registration system. In Ghana, for example, there is continual litigation over clouded titles on former tribal lands.

To convert chaos into order, to make cities workable, to bar bad development and encourage the building of necessary facilities, governments must establish control over the use of land. This is easier said than done. In the days of absolute rulers the procedure was simplicity itself. The king or patriarch merely ordered what he wanted done, whether it was widening a road to make room for his carriage, erecting a castle or building a beautiful city. There was no legal resistance. When, for example, the people of Dublin stubbornly refused to leave their houses on streets that Charles II of England had ordered widened, the king got his way by directing the commissioners to carry off the roofs of the houses. Today governments almost everywhere must reckon with the institution of private ownership of land. Even where the land is publicly owned its use is conditioned by the pressures of the market and public opinion. The control of land use is a formidable problem that no city in the world has yet solved to its complete satisfaction.

Three tools are available for shaping the pattern of land use in cities: regulation, taxation and public acquisition of the land. Let us consider them in turn.

Regulation of the use of land is not a new thing; there were restrictions imposed even in the cities of ancient Babylonia. But the gradual libertarian revolt against the autocracy of rulers generally led to the fixed principle that a man's dwelling, however mean, was his inviolable castle. As William Pitt the Younger declaimed in the 18th century, although storms and rains might enter one's property, "the King of England cannot enter; all his forces dare not cross the threshold of the ruined tenement."

The industrial age eventually forced governments to intervene for the sake of health and safety and establish some control over housing and other city conditions. From the beginning, regulation was expanded until it now includes strict building codes, zoning specifications for land use and even rent controls. Regulation has not, however, proved to be a master key to solution of the problems of improving the urban environment. Although regulations on new buildings restrict objectionable development, they also raise costs and thus put new housing beyond the reach of low-income families. Moreover, in all too many metropolitan communities the zoning power has been used not to ameliorate housing conditions but to exclude the poor from the more attractive living areas.

In the less developed countries regulation is virtually a flat failure as a policy. Often they are unable to enforce restrictions simply because they lack enforcement machinery. In Turkey builders ignored a building code because there were no civil servants who could read their blueprints. In La Paz, the capital of Bolivia, rent-control laws not only are held in contempt by landlords but also terrorize tenants, who fear their landlords might be tempted by the provision that an apartment be decontrolled when its occupant dies! In any case, the underdeveloped countries, the great need of which is to encourage investment in building, are generally unwilling to adopt restrictive regulations that may discourage it.

The taxation of land is a more effective method of controlling its use than regulation is. It can be a potent and versatile instrument for desirable development of urban real estate. Pakistan, for example, has adopted a law (on the advice of a United Nations mission) that imposes penalty taxes on land if it is not built on within a specified period. A few other countries have resorted to the same policy. It is a useful, but far from a common, device for preventing the holding of land for speculative profits; indeed, three centuries ago the colony of New Amsterdam in New York used it to squelch land speculation within the stockade. Furthermore, the taxation of undeveloped land helps governments to finance roads and utilities and to recover some of the rise in land values that accompanies such improvements.

Unfortunately taxation policies, even in the advanced nations, are too confused and fragmented to allow general use of the real estate tax as a social tool. Some countries, particularly former colonies that have recently become independent, do not tax land at all. Others tax it so heavily that home owners are overburdened and investment in land is discouraged. Boston has a real estate tax that amounts to paying 11 percent of the estimated value of the land each year—surely a confiscatory tax. Singapore levies a tax amounting to 36 percent of the gross rent from real property; the result is that the city has no rental dwellings. In all countries, especially in their cities, the use of the taxing power still remains a crude instrument that often serves to retard the city rather than advance it. The development of a proper tax system for our increasingly urbanized society is obviously a major problem that calls for immediate and massive study.

Disillusioned about what can be accomplished by regulation or by taxation, most countries have decided that they must take a direct hand in their own construction or reconstruction. They now acquire land not only for roads, parks, government buildings and the other purposes traditionally recognized as public works but also for industry, commerce, housing, parking and a host of purposes long considered as being in the private domain. In doing so they have adopted a policy (as in urban renewal programs) that a generation ago would have been considered an unthinkable violation of private rights: taking property away from one individual in order to sell it to another [see "The Renewal of Cities," by Nathan Glazer, page 175]. The policy is now accepted as unavoidable if cities are not to fall into unbearable decay. Indeed, it can be justified ethically, because we now live in a world in which land and money are more freely exchangeable. Moreover, of the three forms of land control to which the city may resort—regulation, taxation or purchase—purchase of the property is the only one that compensates the private owner for his deprivation.

The specific objective that launched this sharp innovation in policy was "slum clearance." By painful experience the U.S. and other countries have now learned that there is no magic or easy formula for replacing slums with something better. In the U.S. "clearance" has left many families without housing at the rent they can afford to pay (or in worse housing than they had before). In Lagos, the capital of Nigeria, the story has been more dismal. Soon after the country gained its independence in 1960 the minister of affairs for the capital decided to eliminate the city's slums to improve the nation's image in the eyes of the world. Instead of beginning with the building of a sewer system, as the World Bank had recommended, Lagos on the advice of its foreign consultants set out to demolish a 70-acre slum area. It took 200 helmeted policemen to protect the project against the protests of the displaced residents. By the time the Nigerian government had cleared and rebuilt a third of the land, it had run out of funds and had to stop. The city was left with a few dramatic skyscrapers—but no sewer. Lagos is still drenched with sewage: 85 percent of its schoolchildren have hookworm or roundworm and more than 10 percent of all the deaths in the city are attributed to dysentery or diarrhea.

Slum clearance is still a popular policy in many countries, but a few planners are coming to believe that in the poorer countries "planned slums," if provided with decent sanitary facilities and other minimal necessities, are preferable to costly projects that consume precious capital without rehousing the people who need housing most. Particularly in warm climates, where people spend most of their time outdoors, minimal housing can be built on the city's periphery (often with local materials by the residents themselves) at very low cost, and these will do for a period until they can be improved or replaced by better structures. In cities or countries that cannot afford more ambitious improvements, such shelters may be the most realistic answer to the immediate needs of the rural refugees descending on the cities.

The move of governments into an active role in building or re-

newing cities has raised anew, and in a new form, the ancient issue
of public v. private ownership of land. Each country has its own
views on this question, and it is instructive to compare them. Particularly illuminating is a comparison of the evolution of policies
in the U.S. and the U.S.S.R.

The U.S. emerged as a nation 175 years ago out of what might
be called a land revolution. It offered land to anyone who could
use it and provided firm guaranties of the rights of ownership. Individual ownership of land and home became a more important
force than the Constitution for building democracy. The policy
was succinctly stated by Thomas Jefferson: ". . . as few as possible shall be without a little portion of land. The small landhold-
ers are the most precious part of the state."

This pattern of private ownership has survived, and indeed been
strengthened, during the nation's growth and transition from a
rural to an urban-industrial society. In financial crises and natural
catastrophes the Federal Government has come to the rescue with
massive support to enable people to save their homes, their farms
and their small businesses. Within recent years, thanks to the Federal Housing Administration and other Government aids, individual home ownership has grown to an unprecedented degree.

At the same time the ownership of land by industry and other
large-scale enterprises has become less significant. In fact, many
of these institutions, including chain supermarkets, factories and
giant business organizations housed in skyscrapers, prefer to lease
their sites rather than own them. In addition there has been a
steady enlargement of the lands that may be taken for public use.
Until the end of the 19th century the Federal Government was not
even permitted to buy land for national parks; this precedent was
broken down only when the courts decided that it would be per-
missible to establish the Gettysburg battlefield as a national shrine
and patriotic inspiration. Since then Federal ownership has been
extended into other realms (notably the Tennessee Valley development), but it is still restricted to special projects that are
"Federal purposes." Only the states and cities (the states' crea-
tures) may condemn land for housing and other urban purposes.

The basic tradition of private ownership and private rights
remains strong. The Federal Government is refused any effective
supervision over local zoning or development. The nation is broken

up into more than 210 metropolitan areas, each further fragmented into scores or hundreds of urban and suburban governments that maintain a chaotic hodgepodge of different policies and jealously erect zoning guards against invasion of their communities by unwelcome minorities or income groups. When the Johnson Administration asked Congress to enact legislation that would have authorized the states to acquire land for the building of new towns in metropolitan areas, the proposal was coldly rejected without audible protest from suburban dwellers.

The British, in contrast, have come to believe strongly in public ownership and national control of their urban lands. They were led to this view largely by their need for rebuilding after the war, by congestion in their cities and by concern for preservation of the beauties of their countryside. In the new towns (mostly satellites of the great cities) that Britain has built since the war, it has maintained the principle that the land acquired by the planning agencies must remain in public ownership. At an international meeting on city planning held in Moscow under the auspices of the UN in 1964 the British delegate urged that new towns in all countries adopt that policy. Because the developing countries have been greatly impressed by the achievements of Britain's new-towns program (the plan has become, as one British planner put it, one of Britain's "most substantial exports"), the Moscow conference almost unanimously endorsed the public-ownership policy. The only dissenter was the U.S. delegate; he was promptly denounced by Soviet delegates as a spokesman of capitalism.

What, then, has been the experience of the U.S.S.R.? It has, in fact, considerably modified the abolition of private property that was instituted by the Revolution. Individuals in the U.S.S.R. still may not own land, but they are allowed property rights to their own dachas (suburban or country houses). A Soviet citizen may buy a cooperative apartment, and increasing numbers are doing so. The Soviet government may take over private property for public purposes, but it must pay the owner a fair compensation for the property. In short, the U.S.S.R., like other countries, is slowly coming to recognize the universal longing and need of each person for a place of his own.

It seems altogether likely that policies concerning land ownership will continue to differ substantially from country to country. Some will lean toward predominantly private ownership, some toward "socialist" ownership, others toward a mixture of the two systems. There are countries where the renting tradition prevails (as in Britain) and land ownership has no strong emotional meaning for most of the people. In other countries politicians looking for votes would not hesitate to urge renters to stop paying rent to their governments unless the houses are sold to them. There are still others, such as India, where poverty and crowding make urban home ownership out of the question. Nonetheless, in rich countries and in poor, the desire for a piece of land or dwelling one can call one's own remains an unquenchable human aspiration. More than almost anything else, it spells security and individual integrity, particularly amidst the pressures on privacy and the immensity of the city.

The defiance of the millions of city squatters who are seizing tiny plots of land for themselves is an expression of such a human urge; in some respects many of these squatters are present-day counterparts of the migrants who settled the American West and the Australian hinterland.

In these terms a planner must regard the world's cities as a still unsettled frontier. Their forms, their populations and their uses of land have not by any means hardened into a stable mold. As more land is bought within the urban orbit the form and organization of the metropolis will doubtless change. It would be helpful if we had a few space agencies, appropriately financed, devoting themselves to exploration of how we can make better use of earth space to build better and more comfortable cities.

Transportation in Cities

· JOHN W. DYCKMAN

Urban transportation has to do not only with moving people and goods into, out of and through the city but also with the spatial organization of all human activities within it.

PROBLEMS OF URBAN TRANSPORTATION are not new in the world. In the first century A.D. the municipal government of Rome was obliged to relieve congestion in its streets by restricting vehicular traffic (with the exception of chariots and state vehicles) to the night hours. Rome was then the only truly "big" city in the Western world, however, and for many centuries thereafter its transportation problem remained the exception rather than the rule. It was not until the process of industrialization was well under way in the 19th century that vehicular traffic began to present serious problems in cities. Today descriptions of the conditions of movement in cities express the alarm of the observer with words such as "choke" and "strangle." Not only are there now more big cities; some of them are tending to consolidate into huge megalopolitan networks, further compounding the comparatively elementary difficulties that faced the Romans.

Among the complaints commonly heard about modern systems

of urban transportation are congestion, the overloading of routes and facilities, the overlong trips, the irregularity and inconvenience of those services that are publicly provided and the difficulty of parking private vehicles at desired destinations. These are problems that arise not only out of the sheer size of modern cities but also out of the organization of their land uses, the rhythm of their activities, the balancing of their public services with private rights of access and movement, and the tastes and preferences of their citizens with respect to mode of travel, route, comfort and cost. There is in fact no isolated "transportation problem" in the modern metropolis; there are problems of the spatial organization of human activities, the adaptability of existing facilities and investments, and the needs and aspirations of the people in moving themselves and their goods. For the individual city dweller, nonetheless, the contemporary transportation problem remains in large measure a "traffic" problem.

The origins of the modern traffic problem are rooted in the very nature of industrialization in an open society. For example, the modern journey to work, which accounts for a large part of the urban traffic problem, is the product of a comparatively free choice of residence and place of work, made freer in industrialized societies by the greater number and variety of both. In the early industrial centers of the Western countries workers were grouped in dwellings close to their respective places of work. In the U.S. even employers did not commute long distances but typically drove to work in carriages from houses within convenient reach of their factories.

Improvements in living standards have contributed almost as much as the growth of cities to contemporary urban traffic conditions. Expectations of greater comfort and convenience, as well as the ability to sustain higher costs, have affected the choice of both residence and mode of travel. The transportation plight of cities—at least in the prosperous, developed countries of the world—is a condition people have themselves brought about by taking advantage of individual opportunities. Accordingly if major changes are to be achieved in the present condition of transportation, deliberate individual and collective decisions on the whole question of the quality of urban life must first be made.

The task of an urban transportation system is to move people and goods from place to place. This elementary statement of purpose is useful because it reminds one that the task is defined by the location of the terminal points as well as by the channels of movement. For this reason the problem of urban transportation is one of city layout and planning as well as one of transportation technology.

The city planner's approach to the transportation problem can be viewed as having two aspects: (1) the definition of the tasks and requirements of the system and (2) the devising of socially acceptable and economically feasible means of achieving those objectives. This approach depends on the existence of basic studies of the use of land in cities in order to relate these uses to transportation needs. Fortunately such basic data on land uses have been available in several U.S. cities, notably Philadelphia. Robert Mitchell and Chester Rapkin of the University of Pennsylvania drew on the Philadelphia data for a prototype "city planning" study of urban transportation in 1954. Their thesis was that different types of land use generate different or variable traffic flows. Such work shifted the emphasis from the study of the flows themselves to the study of the land uses that give rise to the flows. It underlined the basic city-planning proposition that traffic can be manipulated by controlling and rearranging the land uses that represent the destinations and purposes of transportation.

This approach—sometimes called the functional approach because it emphasizes the relation between city functions and transportation—has come to dominate large urban transportation studies supported by the U.S. Bureau of Public Roads and other public agencies. The approach has been applied in the Detroit Area Transportation Study, the Chicago Area Transportation Study, the Penn-Jersey Transportation Study and the Tri-State New York Metropolitan Transportation Study. These elaborate investigations (costing approximately $1 per capita in the regions mentioned) have done much to organize existing information about urban transportation, in spite of a heavy preoccupation with automobile traffic and road networks. Surveys of travel behavior are usually made at the homes and places of work of commuters. In addition, the Bureau of Public Roads has long conducted surveys to sample the purposes of householders' trips as well as their actual travel behavior; these data are integrated in the large transportation studies with such information as the addresses of workers by place of work, and sample origins and destinations of travelers en route.

The customary unit of travel—the "trip"—takes many forms, and in these studies the purposes of various kinds of trip must be differentiated. Shopping trips and recreational trips, for example, have many characteristics that distinguish them from trips to and from work. From an analysis of such characteristics the possibility of replacing one mode of travel (perhaps the automobile) by another (perhaps mass transit) can be considered.

The outstanding contributions of the major transportation studies, apart from the accumulation and organization of data, have been (1) the approach to transportation as a comprehensive system of interrelated activities; (2) the recognition of the importance of land uses, demographic and social characteristics and consumer choices in determining transportation requirements; (3) an appreciation of the role of transportation itself in shaping the development of cities and metropolitan areas, and (4) the acceptance of the inevitably metropolitan scale of transportation planning in a society in which daily activities that generate travel move freely across the borders of local government and form the functionally interdependent fabric of the metropolitan region.

In focusing on the whole system of relations between users and facilities these elaborate studies should furnish the material for the solution to the two major problems of urban transportation: how to obtain efficient movement and how to promote new activities. The promotion of new urban activities is the province of city planning, but the city-planning results of the major transportation studies have not yet clearly emerged. The studies reflect the current condition of the planning profession, which is ambivalent toward the automobile and split on the issue of centralization v. dispersal.

The city-forming role of transportation facilities is well known to city planners. The New York subway of 1905 opened up the Bronx; the radiating street-railway systems of the late 19th and early 20th centuries created the working-class suburbs of Boston, Chicago and Philadelphia. Today, of course, expressways are opening up a far greater number of new suburban housing developments and shopping centers than the subway and street railways did.

To many city planners the central contemporary problem is one of conserving cities "as we have known them." These planners be lieve the issue is between centrality and spread, between efficient downtowns and disorganized ones. They see the present use of the automobile for the bulk of urban trips as destroying the amenities of the established downtown by contributing to congestion, eating up real estate for parking and storage, interfering with pedestrian flow and poisoning the air of the central city. Almost equally bad from their standpoint, the automobile makes possible the scattering of residences, of auxiliary commercial facilities and ultimately even of the downtown headquarters function. The planners' views are shared by many realtors holding downtown property, by some established merchants and by civic leaders who see the new emphasis on highway building as inevitably creating competing centers in outlying areas. If we are to have compact cities with centrally located places of work, relatively high-density residential zones, concentration of shopping and public facilities as well as employment, the currently dispersive effects of the automobile will have to be checked.

Other planners, not opposed to dispersal on these grounds, believe the growth of urban population itself is likely to produce a situation in which scale effects rule out present modes of transportation. These observers believe the congestion that will be faced by cities containing upward of 15 million people will be such as to require greatly enlarged capacity for traffic channels, the restriction of vehicles to specialized lanes, controlled timing and phasing of movement and many other adaptations more drastic than those proposed in present transportation plans.

In spite of the fact that every major transportation study has projected an increase in the ownership of automobiles, in the volume of automobile traffic to be accommodated in central cities, in the construction of new expressways and in the spread of metropolitan population, a number of the larger cities in the U.S. are taking steps in the direction of reinvestment or new investment in public mass transportation. In many cases this takes the form of building or expanding subways and related rail systems; in every case a major portion of the system is characterized by fixed routes and separate rights-of-way.

Public transportation systems are frequently a combination of "rapid transit," which uses for high-speed service rights-of-way that are separated by grade crossings, and "local transit," which uses public streets (with or without rail lines) and makes local stops. A truly effective transportation system must offer a full range of service, from the rapid-express system to the local-distribution system. Cities as far apart as San Francisco and Washington intend to build new subways; New York, Chicago and other cities propose to extend their existing systems; in the Northeast particular attention is being given to the problem of resuscitating privately owned commuter railroads and reviving the relation between these roads and the city transit systems. The Federal Government has shown interest in supporting these efforts, but as yet it has mounted no program comparable in scope to its highway-building effort.

City planners and transportation experts have turned to mass-transportation systems at a moment of grave difficulty for the established transportation companies. Transit franchises, which at the turn of the century were prized plums for entrepreneurs and investors, have long since ceased to be notably profitable. In most cases the companies have either been taken over by the cities or have gone out of business. Although the very large cities could scarcely function without transit systems, the systems in these cities too have over the past decade suffered a decline in riders. The share of total commutation accountable to the automobile has risen at the expense of the transit systems.

The difficulties of urban transit companies have been the subject of many studies and need not be recapitulated here. Some of these are difficulties of the systems themselves; others are problems of urban growth and development only slightly related to the systems. The three major difficulties posed for transit by the pattern of growth of our cities are (1) the collection problem, (2) the delivery problem and (3) the "peak" problem.

The collection problem arises largely from the diffuse pattern of urban "sprawl" made possible by widespread ownership of automobiles and ready access to highways. Density of settlement is one of the most important variables in accounting for urban transit

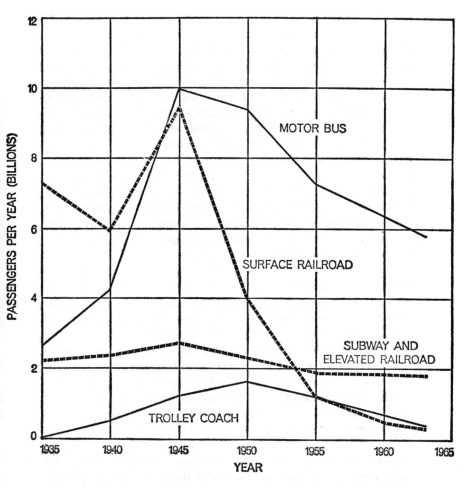

DECLINE IN USE OF MASS TRANSIT in the U.S. since the end of World War II is depicted in this graph. Gasoline and tire rationing, together with booming employment, led to an all-time high in the use of public transit during the war years; since 1945 total transit use has declined nearly 64 percent. In the same period overall route-miles of transit service have increased by 5 percent. The loss of transit riders is largely attributable to enormously increased use of private automobiles for commutation to and from work.

use, and for the performance and profitability of the systems. The New York subways are made possible by the heavy concentration of riders in areas served by the system, just as the system itself makes possible the aggregation of population at these densities. It is obviously difficult for a fixed-route system to collect efficiently in a highly dispersed settlement pattern. Not only is a commuter train unable to collect people door-to-door; the number of stops required to accumulate a payload is increased by a dispersed residential pattern. More stops in turn slow down the performance of the system and hurt it in terms of both operating costs and attractiveness to the rider. The operating disadvantages of the fixed-rail transportation system—relatively low efficiency at low operating speed, the high cost of braking and acceleration, the problems of scheduling, the minimum profitable payload required by fixed costs—all create conflicts between efficient service and low collection densities.

The problem of delivery has been exacerbated by changes in the scale and distribution of activities within the downtown areas as well as the general dispersal of places of work. Within metropolitan areas industries have moved increasingly toward the outskirts in search of larger sites; this movement has tended to disperse places of work and so reduce the usefulness of the highly centered, radial transit systems. Circumferential systems moving through predominantly low-density areas have been less attractive to the transit companies. Within the downtown areas dispersal of places of work and of central points of attraction (brought about by changes such as the shift of a department store to the fashionable fringe of the area) has greatly lengthened that portion of the trip between arrival at the terminal and arrival at the final destination. The lengthening of the walk or taxi ride from station to destination has made the whole transit ride less attractive. These developments can be summed up in the observation that the general dispersal of activities and functions within metropolitan areas has made the fixed-rail system less efficient in point-to-point delivery of passengers.

The "peak" problem arises almost entirely from the organization of journeys in time. For many transit companies 80 percent of the volume of travel is concentrated in 20 hours of the week. This results in the underutilization of rolling stock and other

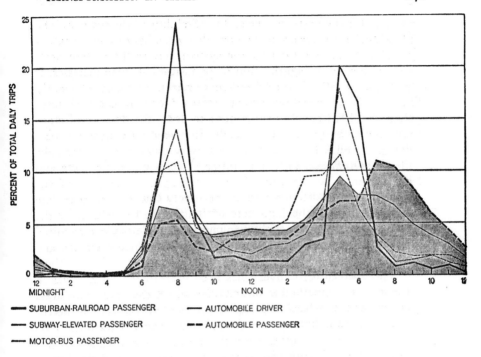

PERCENT OF TOTAL DAILY TRIPS

■■■ SUBURBAN-RAILROAD PASSENGER   ■■■ AUTOMOBILE DRIVER

■■■ SUBWAY-ELEVATED PASSENGER   ■■ ■■ AUTOMOBILE PASSENGER

■■■ MOTOR-BUS PASSENGER

"PEAK" PROBLEM is more acute for public-transit system (top 3 lines in key curves) than for private automobiles (bottom 2 lines in key curves). For many transit companies 80 percent of the volume of travel is concentrated in 20 hours of the week. Such sharp peaks lead to high operating costs, since the capacity for meeting peak loads without breakdown is far in excess of the average capacity of the system. The source of this difficulty is the fact that mass transit is increasingly confined to serving commuter journeys. The concentration of journeys in narrower bands of time has accompanied the movement toward fewer workdays in the week and less work in shifts. Data for charts were drawn from Chicago Area Transportation Study.

equipment necessary for meeting peak loads. The source of this difficulty is the fact that mass transit is increasingly confined to serving commuter journeys. The concentration of journeys in narrower bands of time has been a steadily evolving phenomenon, accompanying the movement toward fewer workdays in the week and less work in shifts.

It is axiomatic to the performance of any system—transportation or otherwise—that sharp peaks lead to high operating costs. The capacity needed for meeting peak loads without breakdown of the system is far in excess of the average capacity required by the system. The need for excess capacity is aggravated by the fact that in transportation accounting the obsolescence cycle and the amortization cycle are out of phase: mass-transportation systems in cities are rarely able to amortize investments in rolling stock and equipment before they are obsolete as a result of technical competition, of shifts in land use or of changes in employment patterns.

Finally, a whole set of factors arising from changes in consumer tastes and expectations have worked to the disadvantage of the fixed-rail system. Comfort, convenience, privacy, storage capacity, guaranteed seating, freedom from dependence on scheduled departure times and a number of intangible satisfactions all favor the use of private automobiles.

In view of the marked advantages of the automobile over other types of carrier, what can the public-transit system be expected to do to alter the present drift in commuter habits? Under what conditions would the transit system be able to compete with the automobile? The engineering efficiency of trains, which can move many times more people and much more cargo for a given road space and energy output than automobiles can, has persistently held out the promise that mass transportation would lower costs. One may ask, however: Costs for whom? Real costs, out-of-pocket costs to users and public costs have all been cited from time to time to make points for and against mass transit. It is particularly important to distinguish the public costs of the respective operations from the private costs and the average costs from the so-called marginal costs.

A recent study by economists at the RAND Corporation concluded that the automobile is competitive with other available modes of travel to work in large American cities. Under the assumptions made by these economists—including a relatively high rate for the driver's or passenger's time—it appears that the one-way hourly cost is lower for the automobile than for most competing modes of travel up to about 15 miles of commuting distance from door to door. In the framework of this analysis the behavior of commuters who choose to commute by automobile is rational.

When one compares the average cost per mile of automobile operation against the cost of transit fares per ride, the comparison may be misleading. The average cost of operating an automobile driven about 10,000 miles a year is close to 10 cents per mile. The marginal cost (the daily out-of-pocket operating cost) is much lower. A sizable fraction of the cost of operating an automobile lies of course in depreciation, insurance, registration, taxes and other fixed-cost items. Gasoline and oil account for only about 15 percent of the total cost. The cost of parking, which might be significant if it were entirely passed on to the consumer at the point of destination, is frequently subsidized by private merchants and public authorities or is provided free by the community on the street. Similarly, the rights-of-way provided in highway programs are financed by gasoline taxes paid by all users, so that long journeys help to subsidize the shorter in-city trips.

As long as private incomes continue to rise, some substitution of private automobile travel for transit is probably inevitable under present competitive conditions. In analyzing the findings of the Detroit Area Transportation Study, John Kain, then at RAND, related much of the change in transit use in Michigan to changes in median family incomes of Michigan residents. His findings disposed him to the view that changes in income were more important in the decline in transit use than deteriorating service. In sum, although the automobile is not a technically elegant solution to the urban transportation problem, it is a socially engaging one because of its adaptability, social prestige and acceptability.

Given these realities, what strategies are being developed for dealing with the overall problem of urban transportation? The two "pure" strategies and (1) all-out accommodation of the automobile and (2) a strategy of banning the automobile from the center city and replacing it on a large scale with rail transit as a mode of journey-to-work travel. Between these two positions are numerous mixed strategies.

Europeans, who are on the verge of entering the automobile age that has enveloped the U.S., have not as yet reacted so strongly to the automobile and are given to accommodative strategies. A firm statement of this view, albeit one tinged with ambivalence and irony, is to be found in the report entitled *Traffic in Towns*, prepared for the British government by Colin Buchanan. The Buchanan report proposes a general theory of traffic based on separation of express and local motor traffic, pedestrian traffic and certain freight movements. Buchanan holds that potential urban amenity is measured by the volume of traffic, since traffic is a measure of the use of buildings and spaces. His proposal for downtown London is based on a vertical separation of traffic: expressways are sunk below street level or are completely automobile subways, the street level is chiefly given over to the storage of vehicles, and pedestrians are lifted to a mezzanine level above the storage level. The principle is the same as the old architectural notion of arcaded shops above the major service lanes.

Although the presuppositions of the Buchanan report, as much as its analyses, lead to a drastic reshaping of cities to accommodate the automobile, similar efforts on a more modest scale are already to be seen in many of the large cities of the world. The downtowns of major U.S. cities have been attempting to adjust to the increasing number of automobiles by various internal adaptations. The process of adaptation has been going on for many years, with the widening of streets, the construction of garage spaces, the building of expressways to speed the exit and entry of cars, and alternating permission to park with restrictions on parking. Large investments in underpasses, bridges, tunnels and ramps have been made in order to integrate the local street systems with the high-speed expressways and to reduce local bottlenecks in the increasing flow of cars.

Calculations made by Ira Lowry of RAND and the University of California at Los Angeles on the basis of the Pittsburgh Transportation Study suggest that gains in transportation efficiency resulting from improved routes and automobile-storage capacity are almost immediately absorbed by the further dispersal of places of work and particularly of residences. This dispersal enables the consumer to indulge his preference for more living space; it also increases the advantage of the automobile over the fixed-route system, and it does not significantly relieve the center-city traffic problem. To borrow a concept from economics, in motoring facilities there is a "Say's law" of accommodation of use to supply: Additional accommodation creates additional traffic. The opening of a freeway designed to meet existing demand may eventually increase that demand until congestion on the freeway increases the travel time to what it was before the freeway existed.

The case for supplementary transportation systems, such as mass transit, arises from the conviction that measures to accommodate the demands of the automobile are approaching the limit of their effectiveness. The primary aim of improved transit systems is to relieve the conditions brought about by the success of the automobile. The issue for many years to come will not be trains v. automobiles but how to balance the two systems, and it may lead to new designs in which both systems complement each other.

The very scale of the effort to transform our cities to accommodate the automobile has, in view of the problems created by such investment, raised serious doubts in the minds of public officials and transportation experts about the efficacy of making further investments of this kind. The cost of building urban freeways in the interstate system has averaged $3.7 million per mile. This is not the entire real cost, however. Freeways are prodigal space-users that remove sizable tracts of land from city tax rolls. Among other costly consequences are the need for storage space for vehicles brought by freeways to the center city, for elaborate traffic-control systems and for the policing of vehicles. Freeway construction frequently displaces large numbers of urban residents; the freeway program accounts for the biggest single share of the residential relocation load resulting from public construction in the U.S. Moreover, automobiles are a prime contributor to air pollution, which can be viewed as the result of private use of a public air sewer over a central city by motorists from the entire metropolitan area [see "The Metabolism of Cities," by Abel Wolman, page 156].

These aspects of automobile transport in our cities have intensified public interest in alternative schemes and have expanded the political appeal of such schemes. At government levels a great deal of support has been mustered for the strengthening of rail systems, both local transit systems and the suburban lines of interstate railroads. Privately, however, consumers continue to vote for the use of the automobile. In view of this tension between public objectives and private choices, the San Francisco Bay Area Rapid Transit District (BARTD) commands special attention.

At roughly the same time that the Buchanan report in Britain

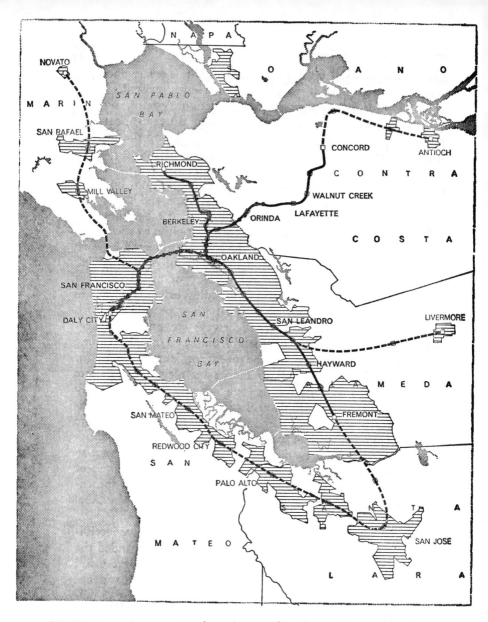

BAY AREA RAPID TRANSIT DISTRICT (BARTD) currently embraces three metropolitan Bay Area counties: San Francisco, Alameda and Contra Costa. Although early studies envisioned five inner Bay counties in the system, San Mateo County withdrew from the plan by 1962 and Marin County, joined to San Francisco by the thin thread of the Golden Gate Bridge, was judged too difficult to serve under present conditions. The 75 miles of track expected to be in operation by 1971 are indicated by the heavy solid line (underground sections are indicated by dotted portion while the solid portions indicate surface or elevated sections). Possible future extensions of the system are indicated by the broken line. Squares denote stations with parking facilities; circles denote stations without parking.

found no reasonable competitive alternative to the automobile, the voters of three counties of the San Francisco Bay Area committed themselves to support the largest bond issue ever undertaken for an urban transportation system. The San Francisco Bay Area Rapid Transit experiment has aroused international interest on a number of counts. Most important perhaps is the fact that this is the first wholly new public-transit system to be built in the U.S. in 50 years and the first openly to challenge the automobile-transportation system in the era marked by the ascendancy of the automobile and the freeway. Almost equally important is the fact that this project is being undertaken as the result of the decision of citizens of a metropolitan area—for the most part automobile owners—to tax themselves to bring an attractive transit alternative into existence. For various reasons one cannot assume an overwhelming consumer mandate, but the actions of the electorate of the three metropolitan Bay Area counties that finally formed the district is remarkable on the American local-government scene, where the assumption of responsibility for transit by voters is, to say the least, unusual.

The Bay Area mass-transit undertaking is the outcome of more than 10 years of major public planning and study of the transportation needs in the region. The earlier studies envisioned participation of at least the seven inner Bay counties in the system; the Bay Area Rapid Transit District created by the California legislature in 1957 would have allowed the participation of five counties. By the time the proposed district was brought before the voters in November, 1962, however, it had been reduced to three counties: San Francisco, Alameda and Contra Costa. San Mateo County, whose Southern Pacific commuter trains serve the older suburbs that generated the bulk of commuting to San Francisco's financial district in an earlier era, withdrew from the plan. Marin County, joined to the city by the thin thread of the Golden Gate Bridge, was judged too difficult to serve under present conditions. The district comprising the three counties was authorized by the voters of those counties to issue $792 million in bonds.

The BARTD system, which is expected to be in operation by 1971, is to be an electric rail system with elevated tracks over some of its routes and subways over others. It is hoped that it will provide technically advanced, comfortable, high-speed commuting that will divert peak-hour travel from automobiles to its trains. To do this it will stress comfort and speed (notably speed; unless the commuter can save appreciable amounts of time he will not easily be diverted). Existing mass-transit systems find it hard to achieve average speeds exceeding 20 miles per hour over the whole of their run; the Bay Area trains will aim at average speeds of 40 to 50 miles per hour and maximum speeds of 80 miles per hour. To attain such average speeds BARTD will operate what is primarily an express system with widely spaced stations fed by buses and automobiles.

In order to be convenient, the express service must be frequent. At present a maximum interval between trains of 15 to 20 minutes at any time of day is contemplated. The proposed interval between trains during hours of peak traffic is 90 seconds. Although slightly less frequent than some rail lines (for example parts of the London subway system at peak), this is very frequent service by American standards; it will be aided by fully automatic controls. A critical factor in the interval between trains is the length of station platforms; this length limits the speed of loading. The BARTD planners hope to have platforms 700 feet long, the longest in the world with the exception of the continuous platforms in the Chicago subway. The maximum interval of 15 to 20 minutes, maintained by varying the number of cars to match anticipated loads, will reduce the number of trains less markedly than would be the case in other transit operations. The BARTD planners believe that in rapid-transit equipment the process of technical obsolescence may be so rapid as to outweigh the fixed costs of wear; thus it will pay, in terms of overall performance, to use the equipment more frequently. If waiting times ranging from 15 to 20 minutes can be maintained around the clock, the BARTD operation will in fact be a suburban rail system with some of the characteristics of local transit. This performance would enable BARTD to avoid the inconvenient schedules that plague the traditional commuter lines, while still offering the high speed and comfort needed to serve effectively the greater distances of commutation characteristic of the present pattern of metropolitan settlement.

The BARTD system will necessarily be expensive. The basic rider's fare has been set in advance planning at 25 cents, with increments based on distance and an average commuter cost of $1 per trip. Fares are expected to cover the operating costs, although the district has some flexibility in case of shortfall. The cost of tunneling under San Francisco Bay will be met by funds diverted from the automobile tolls of the Bay Bridge Authority, under the reasonable expectations that (1) the transit system will help to relieve the overload on the bridges at peak hours and (2) the transit system will not result in a diversion of automobiles so great as to impair revenues from the bridge tolls. With the exception of certain improvements that will be paid for by the cities affected, and some Federal grants for planning and testing new equipment, the remainder of the capital cost will be met from the bond issues. With the bond vote the property owners of the participating counties made themselves available for such additional taxes as would be necessary for building the system. Over a period of time, as costs rise and the system encounters unforeseen difficulties, taxpayers in the member counties could conceivably be saddled with high annual costs. In spite of the fact that at least some property owners will benefit greatly from the existence of the system and that all commuters, drivers as well as riders, will share in a more efficient transportation operation, the real estate taxation base is likely to provoke future political reaction. In this event the more equitable Federal Tax base may offer the most promising relief.

BARTD is staking much on the enthusiasm of its future riders. Its case for that support rests on speed, frequency of service, comfort and convenience resulting from attractive cars, easy ticket handling and other "human engineering" factors. It hopes to make commuting by train as pleasurable for some riders as surveys of commuters tell us driving is for others. As an answer to the general problem of urban transportation, however, it has grave shortcomings to match its great promise.

Perhaps the most significant feature of the BARTD approach is its concentration on the portion of the problem it considers to be crucial: the diversion of some of the peak-hour longer-range commuters. This is certainly an important part of the urban transportation problem in many large cities, particularly in California. It is not the whole problem, however, and some features of the Bay Area system raise doubts about its impact on the total transportation problem of the area.

BARTD must improve its prospects for solving the distribution and collection problems that are the persistent vexations of fixed-rail systems. For its door-to-door service the system depends on connections with the private automobile. A "car park" system, which is proposed to encourage park-and-ride trips, is BARTD's answer, but as it is presently planned this system may not be adequate. Unless the commuter is certain of a parking place at the station, he must either depend on "kiss and ride" assistance—a ride with his wife—or make an earlier decision to park downtown if the station car park is full. Delivery of passengers in San Francisco, Oakland and other business and industrial districts is a similarly serious problem. San Francisco has traditionally been favored by the limited physical scale of its downtown area; the area is compact and densely populated, and it has high intensity of urban activities within a short walk of central points. Oakland, however, is less concentrated. In general two factors work against an easy solution of the delivery problem. One is that downtown areas are spreading; the other is that, as industries seek lower-density sites away from the downtown area, there is a sizable volume of reverse commuting.

The local-transit portions of the BARTD system and its subsidiary feeder-distributor arrangements have thus far received the least consideration. The majority of the downtown workers live in the cities, on the local-transit part of the system, and a sizable number of middle-income and lower-income factory workers commute from moderately priced rental areas in the center city to jobs in suburban areas. The latter are likely to find the trip from the downtown end of the BARTD line to their jobs a difficult one, and the former are likely to find the spacing of the stations inconvenient for the length of trip required. Within the downtown areas there is as yet too little attention to the devices needed to get passengers from the debarkation platform to their destination. Moving sidewalks, local bus connections, jitneys and other devices may have to be carefully integrated into a planned distribution system. At present the most effective distribution systems at downtown terminals are vertical ones making use of high-speed elevators, as in the Pan Am Building above Grand Central Station in New York. The fast, free elevator ride, however, is made possible by the real estate values of the location; as far as the rail system is concerned it is simply a device for capitalizing on the "point to point" features of the fixed-rail line.

If it is not necessary to move passengers too great a distance to and from the station, the passenger conveyor belt—an elevator turned on its side—may prove to be an important adjunct to the rail system. The continuous conveyor belt is a most efficient transportation device (whose possibilities for the movement of freight have not yet been fully tapped in the U.S.). In passenger use its efficiency depends on the length of the trip and, to a lesser degree, on the route and on the means of getting on and off the belt. Belts currently in operation carry as many as 7,000 person per hour in a 42-inch lane. When one considers that a contemporary expressway lane carries only a third of that number, the performance of the belt is promising. Present conveyor belts, however, go only one and a half to two miles per hour. At this low speed it is necessary to keep the ride short in order to hold down total travel time.

The transit-system terminal runs into trouble when the distance the passenger must walk exceeds 1,500 feet. If the passenger is not to spend more than 10 minutes on a belt (an excessive time with respect to the shorter overall journey), the speed must be pushed above 150 feet per minute, or close to two miles per hour; speeds over three miles per hour make it difficult for some passengers to step on and off the belt. With increased use of conveyor belts in airports and parking areas, however, advances in loading and unloading them can be expected.

The fact remains that the moving walkway is a point-to-point device and inherently inflexible. Given the high cost of its installation and the risk of shifting demand in the downtown area, it may be less attractive than the more flexible small bus or car. Failure to develop effective devices at the ends of the trip could jeopardize the success of the BARTD operation; a greater emphasis on securing a cheap, flexible system for quick delivery of discharged passengers at their destination will be needed as the rapid-transit portion of the system moves closer to operation.

If the problem of matching the service to points of origin and destination cannot be solved, the BARTD system may turn out to be an interim rather than a long-range solution to the Bay Area transportation problem. The BARTD lines will form a double-track system relying on third-rail power and using relatively conventional railroad cars. BARTD's principal departure from standardization—a wider rail gauge—promises a somewhat smoother ride than the conventional gauge but has the serious drawback of impeding integration with the Southern Pacific Railroad system in the event that San Mateo County is brought into the district. The BARTD decision to use wide-gauge tracks is at variance with plans in Philadelphia, Chicago, and New York to push for the integration of portions of the traditional railroad commuter lines with local transit operations.

Experts who are not sanguine about the role of rail systems in moving people from door to door are advocating more drastically altered systems. Any mass-transit system depends on the principle of specialized vehicles and routes. Automobile expressways can be designed to offer specialized routes, such as separate rights-of-way and separate levels. Rail transit offers the same in addition to a specialized vehicle: the train. A Cornell Aeronautical Laboratory report for the Department of Commerce urged consideration of a system that would combine the automobile's vehicular versatility with some of rail transit's advantages for part of a typical trip. Such a system would be an automatically controlled automobile freeway; it might be able to push the capacity of the freeway close to that of the rail system without sacrificing the collection-and-distribution advantages of the individually operated vehicle.

Some of the engineers who have considered the design of an automatic freeway favor the use of small, electrically powered cars that can be automatically controlled in certain zones, coupled and uncoupled without danger or discomfort and conveniently stored at their destination. The case for electric power is made on the grounds of reducing the air pollution associated with emission of hydrocarbons by internal-combustion engines and on the grounds of the improving economy of battery-powered vehicles in stop-and-go driving. The case for a coupling device is based on the desire to secure automatic control on expressways and storage in central business districts. Since electric cars designed for intra-metropolitan use would be smaller than conventional cars, less space would be needed in which to park them.

Such systems were of course not available to BARTD, although they may be useful in future planning of transportation. The

BARTD system is potentially the most advanced mass-transit system in the U.S. and at the same time, in the words of the planning critic Allan Temko, "something which is patently less than the best that 20th-century technology makes possible." Perhaps the transit of the future will be automatic, coupled private vehicles; perhaps it will take the form of improvements in present train technology, with air-cushioned trains riding above the roadbed, sped by linear-induction motors; perhaps it will appear as a system of passenger or automobile carriers traveling at high speed in pneumatic tunnels.

Whatever the vehicular technology, it will be well to recall Wilfred Owen's caution in 1957 that "the so-called transportation problem is only half a transportation problem. Half the problem is to supply the facilities for moving. The other half is creating an environment in which the transportation system has a chance to work." In this respect it is unfortunate that the BARTD transportation plan has, for a variety of historical reasons, preceded an effective plan of metropolitan land use. The success of BARTD will depend partly on shifts in population density and land use in the region, and the operations of BARTD (along with other elements of the regional transportation system, such as the expressways) will help to shape the development of the region.

As presently constituted, the system is highly "centered" on San Francisco, with Oakland as a subcenter. Although San Francisco is the historic center of the area, it was genuinely central for transportation only in the period in which the Bay Area depended on seaborne traffic. In the rail era Oakland was more central for transportation lines, and today the Bay Area has the form of a linear city broadly looping south down the San Francisco Peninsula, through San José and northward around through Fremont, Oakland and Berkeley. In the expressway system San José is more central, but San José is now not even in the BARTD system. The region-forming role of BARTD is essentially conservative and is aimed at the preservation of an erstwhile centrality of San Francisco. To succeed in this effort it must overcome strong centrifugal tendencies in the growth of the region. In an era in which technology is continually providing opportunities for decentralization (by allowing the substitution of communication for transportation, of message flows for person flows) and is reducing the relative cost of transportation, thereby diminishing the importance of the central place, this task may be increasingly difficult.

The real test of BARTD and its successors in other regions will be whether or not they can adapt effectively to the megalopolitan pattern of settlement. The problem of intramegalopolitan transport will increasingly be one of effective intercity, as well as intracity, links. If, for example, intercity rail transit can achieve maximum speeds of more than 100 miles per hour and average speeds of more than 70 miles per hour, it can be as effective as other modes of transportation, including air travel, for distances up to about 300 miles. Within megalopolitan areas, as their extent increases, we may find that it is desirable to re-create a modern version of the old interurban electric system that once tied Middle Western cities together. One advantage of such a system is that it would call for the regional planning of routes, stations and schedules; if transportation can create development values, it can also withhold them and mold the development of the region.

As cities evolve into supercities, transportation planners must reckon with future urban form and scale as well as with future technology. The change is not occurring overnight. Even now, however, we have clear evidence of population overspill into the interstices between cities, of the growth of industry in outlying, low-density portions of the linear connections between cities, of the stabilization of employment in the central business districts, of the growth of circumferential and loop connections between employment centers and of the growing share of metropolitan employment and business outside the central city.

If the transportation systems serving these new agglomerations are to grow out of the present systems, the emphasis will have to be placed on the consolidation and rationalization of present operations, on the building of links now missing in the networks and on the development of new systems that will complement existing ones. To provide one example, in the BARTD region the Golden Gate crossing is vital to the integration of Marin County into the district and could become the focus for technical work on lightweight cars that could be suspended from monorails on the existing bridge. An important step in the recognition of the modern urban transportation problem is represented by recent proposals in Boston, New York, Philadelphia and Chicago to integrate various transit companies, railroad operations, bridge and tunnel authorities and other elements in local transport. Coordinated development of highways and rail transit, of local and express service, of private automobiles, trucks and buses will be the hallmark of any forward-looking transportation plan. In this chapter there has been little mention of freight; the facilities for handling freight have in many instances far outstripped the performance of those for handling passengers.

Finally, of course, transportation planning will proceed in the context of social choice and individual values, which in the U.S set the priorities for planning and also the limits on it. Government officials have decided to push the development of supersonic air craft well in advance of decisions to develop the high-speed sur face facilities that will be needed to connect the increasingly re mote airports with the destinations of passengers and cargo—even though 2,000-mile-per-hour aircraft will need 300-mile-per-hour ground connections to make any economic sense. Yet we may have both before we have effective integration of the Long Island Rail Road, the New York City subway system and the Triborough Bridge Authority.

The Metabolism of Cities

• ABEL WOLMAN

In the U.S. today attention is focused on shortages of water and the pollution of water and air. There is plenty of water, but supplying it requires foresight. Pollution calls for public economic decisions.

THE METABOLIC REQUIREMENTS of a city can be defined as all the materials and commodities needed to sustain the city's inhabitants at home, at work and at play. Over a period of time these requirements include even the construction materials needed to build and rebuild the city itself. The metabolic cycle is not completed until the wastes and residues of daily life have been removed and disposed of with a minimum of nuisance and hazard. As man has come to appreciate that the earth is a closed ecological system, casual methods that once appeared satisfactory for the disposal of wastes no longer seem acceptable. He has the daily evidence of his eyes and nose to tell him that his planet cannot assimilate without limit the untreated wastes of his civilization.

No one study could describe the complete metabolism of the modern city. Moreover, many of the metabolic inputs such as food, fuel, clothing, durable goods, construction materials and electric energy present no special problem. Their supply is handled routinely, in part through local initiative and in part through large organizations (public or private) that operate about as effectively in one city as another. I shall be concerned therefore with three metabolic problems that have become more acute as cities have grown larger and whose solution rests almost entirely in the hands of the local administrator. Although he can call on many outside sources for advice, he must ultimately provide solutions fashioned to the unique needs of his own community. These three problems are the provision of an adequate water supply, the effective disposal of sewage and the control of air pollution.

That these three problems vary widely from city to city and that they are being managed with widely varying degrees of success is obvious to anyone who reads a daily newspaper. It is ironic, for example, that New York City, which houses the nation's (if not the world's) greatest concentration of managerial talent, should be running short of water while billions of gallons of fresh water flow past it to the sea. It is not easy for people living in arid countries, or even for those living in the southwestern part of the U.S., to have much sympathy with New York's plight.

During the summer of 1965, while New Yorkers were watching their emptying reservoirs and hoping for rain, Californians were busy building an aqueduct that would carry water some 440 miles from the Sacramento River, near Sacramento, to Los Angeles and other cities in the southern part of the state. And thanks to earlier examples of foresight, people in southern California were watering their lawns and filling their swimming pools without restriction, while in New York and New Jersey lawns were dying and pools stood empty. In the water-rich Middle Atlantic states water shortages are largely the result of delayed action and failures of management—sometimes exacerbated by political jockeying.

If American cities have had such unequal success in supplying their citizens with water, it is hardly surprising that some should have an even less satisfactory record in controlling water and air pollution, areas in which the incentives for providing remedies are much weaker than those that motivate the supplying of water. To make matters worse, pollutants of water and air often do not respect state boundaries. For example, the wastes of five states—Michigan, Indiana, Ohio, Pennsylvania and New York—have contributed to the accelerated pollution of Lake Erie. "The lake,"

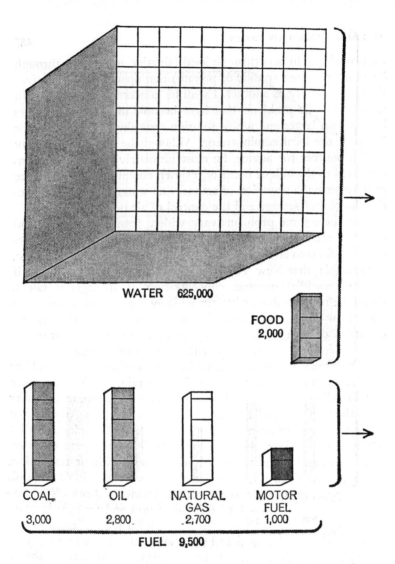

WATER 625,000

FOOD
2,000

COAL
3,000

OIL
2,800

NATURAL
GAS
2,700

MOTOR
FUEL
1,000

FUEL 9,500

METABOLISM OF A CITY involves countless input-output transactions. This chart concentrates on three inputs common to all cities, namely water, food and fuel, and three outputs, sewage, solid refuse and air pollutants. Each item is shown in tons per day for a hypothetical U.S. city with a population of one million. Water, which enters the city silently and unseen, overshadows all other inputs in volume. More than .6 ton (150 gallons) must be supplied to each inhabitant every day. After about 20 percent of the water has been diverted to lawns and other unrecoverable uses, it returns, contaminated, to the city's sewers. The city's most pervasive nuisance, air pollution, is accounted for chiefly by the combustion of fuels. (If refuse is burned in incinerators,

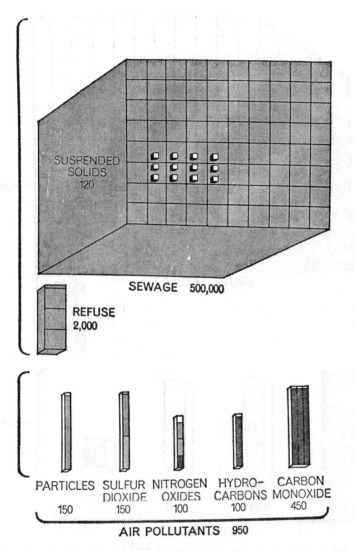

SUSPENDED
SOLIDS
120

SEWAGE 500,000

REFUSE
2,000

PARTICLES SULFUR NITROGEN HYDRO- CARBON
DIOXIDE OXIDES CARBONS MONOXIDE
150 150 100 100 450

AIR POLLUTANTS 950

it can also contribute heavily, but that contribution is not included here.) The various air pollutants are keyed by shadings to the fuel responsible. Most of the particle emission (soot and fly ash) is produced by coal burned in electric power plants, and in well-designed plants more than 90 percent of the particles can be removed from the stack gases. For this hypothetical city one may assume that 135 of the 150 tons of particles produced by all fuel consumers are removed before they reach the atmosphere. All other emissions, however, pollute the atmosphere in the volumes shown. Sulfur dioxide is based on use of domestic fuels of average sulfur content.

according to the U.S. Public Health Service, "has deteriorated in quality at a rate many times greater than its normal aging process." The fourth-largest and shallowest of the five Great Lakes, Lake Erie is the main water supply for 10 million U.S. citizens as well as for the huge industrial complex that extends for 300 miles along the lake's southern shore from Detroit to Buffalo. The combination of treated and partially treated municipal sewage and industrial wastes that enters Lake Erie directly, and also reaches it indirectly through a network of rivers, has disrupted the normal cycle of aquatic life, has led to the closing of a number of beaches and has materially changed the commercial fishing industry. In August 1965 the five states, in consultation with the Public Health Service, reached agreement on a major program of pollution abatement.

Although engineers concerned with water supply, sewage disposal and air pollution are accustomed to thinking in terms of large volumes, few laymen quite appreciate the quantities of water, sewage and air pollutants involved in the metabolism of a modern city. One may express these quantities in the form of an input-output chart for a hypothetical American city of one million population. The input side of the chart will show the requirements in tons per day of water, food and fuels of various kinds. The output side will show the metabolic products of that input in terms of sewage, solid refuse and air pollutants. The quantities thus shown will be a millionfold multiplication of the daily requirements of the average city dweller. Directly or indirectly he uses about 150 gallons (1,250 pounds) of water, four pounds of food and 19 pounds of fossil fuels. This is converted into roughly 120 gallons of sewage (which assumes 80 percent recovery of the water input), four pounds of refuse (which includes food containers and miscellaneous rubbish) and 1.9 pounds of air pollutants, of which automobiles, buses and trucks account for more than half.

As of 1963 about 150 million out of 189 million Americans, or 80 percent, lived in some 22,000 communities served by 19,200 waterworks. These 150 million people used about 23 billion gallons per day (b.g.d.), a volume that can be placed in perspective in several ways. In 1960 the amount of water required for all purposes in the U.S. was about 320 b.g.d., or roughly 15 times the municipal demand. The biggest user of water is irrigation, which in 1960 took about 140 b.g.d. Steam electric utilities used about 98 b.g.d. and industry about 60 b.g.d. Since 1960 the total U.S. water demand has risen from about 320 b.g.d. to an estimated 370 b.g.d., of which municipalities take about 25 b.g.d.

Thus municipalities rank as the smallest of the four principal users of water. Although it is true that water provided for human consumption must sometimes meet standards of quality that need not be met by water used in agriculture or industry, nevertheless throughout most of the U.S. farms, factories and cities frequently draw water from a common supply.

For the country as a whole the supply of available water is enormous: about 1,200 b.g.d. This is the surface runoff that remains from an average daily rainfall of some 4,200 b.g.d. About 40 percent of the total precipitation is utilized where it falls, providing water to support vegetation of economic value: forests, farm crops and pasturelands. Another 30 percent evaporates directly from the soil or returns to the atmosphere after passing through vegetation that has no particular economic value except insofar as it may prevent erosion of the land.

It is obvious that one cannot expect to capture and put to use every drop of the 1,200 b.g.d. flowing to the sea. The amount that can be captured depends on what people are willing to pay for water. One recent estimate places the economically available supply at somewhat less than half the total, or 560 b.g.d. In my opinion this estimate is too conservative; I would suggest a figure of at least 700 b.g.d.

Even this volume would be inadequate by the year 2000—if all the water withdrawn for use were actually consumed. This, however, is not the case now and will not be then; only a small fraction of the water withdrawn is consumed. In 1960 "consumptive use," as it is called, amounted to about 90 b.g.d. of the 320 b.g.d. withdrawn. Most of the remaining 230 b.g.d. was returned after use to the source from which it was taken, or to some other body of water (in some instances the ocean). A small fraction of the used water was piped into the ground to help maintain local water tables.

Estimates by a Senate Select Committee a few years ago projected a consumptive use of about 120 b.g.d. in 1980 and of nearly

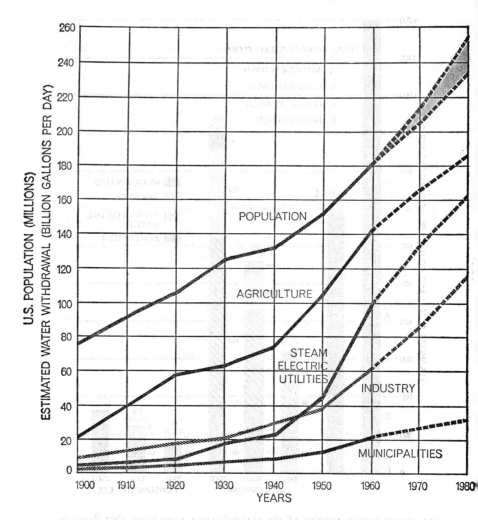

U.S. WATER REQUIREMENTS will be 53 percent greater in 1980 than in 1960, according to the most recent estimates of the Department of Commerce. Virtually all water used by agriculture is for irrigation; nearly 60 percent of all irrigated land in the U.S. is in five Western states (California, Texas, Colorado, Idaho and Arizona) where water tends to be scarcest. Steam power plants need water in huge amounts simply to condense steam. In 1960 municipalities used about 22 billion gallons per day (b.g.d.), which represented only about 7 percent of the total water withdrawal of about 320 b.g.d. The important distinction between water "withdrawal" and "consumptive use" is shown in the illustration on the next page.

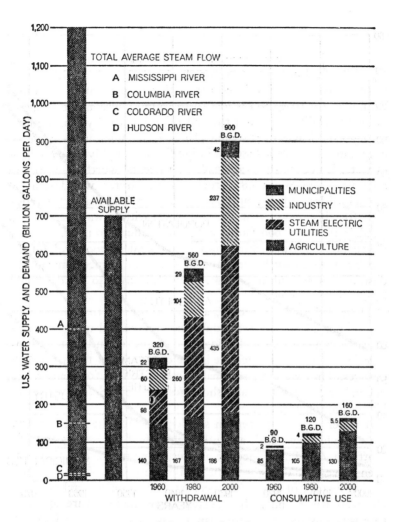

U.S. WATER SUPPLY consists of the approximately 1,200 b.g.d. that flows to the sea through the nation's waterways. This is the streamflow that results from an average precipitation volume of some 4,200 b.g.d. About 70 percent of all precipitation returns to the atmosphere without ever reaching the sea. The average flow of four important rivers is marked on the streamflow column. The author estimates that about 700 b.g.d. of the total streamflow can be made available for use at cost acceptable to consumers. The estimates of water withdrawal and consumptive use for 1980 and 2000 are (with slight rounding) those published a few years ago by a Senate Select Committee. The 1980 estimate is 13 percent higher than that of the Department of Commerce shown in the preceding illustration. "Consumptive use" represents the amount of water withdrawn that subsequently becomes unavailable for reuse. Except for irrigation, consumptive use of water is and will remain negligible. Thus a 700-b.g.d. supply should easily meet a 900-b.g.d. demand.

160 b.g.d. in the year 2000, when total demand may reach 900 b.g.d. Agriculture accounts for the biggest consumptive use of water. It is conservatively estimated that 60 percent of the water employed for irrigation is lost to the atmosphere as the result of evaporation directly from the soil or indirectly by transpiration through the leaves of growing plants. (The amount of water incorporated into plant tissue is insignificant; roughly 1,000 gallons of water is needed to produce about 10 cents' worth of crop.) In contrast, from 80 to 98 percent of the water withdrawn by municipalities, industry and electric utilities is available for reuse. It is for this reason that the projected withdrawal rate of 900 b.g.d. in the year 2000 should not prove difficult to meet, whether the economically available supply is 560 b.g.d. or 700 b.g.d. Of the 900 b.g.d. that may be required in A.D. 2000 to meet human, industrial and agricultural needs, approximately 740 b.g.d. should be available for reuse.

These estimates, moreover, are pessimistic in that they make only minor allowances for reductions in industrial or agricultural demands as a result of technological changes and in that they provide for no significant increase in the cost of water to hasten such changes. Thus we must reasonably conclude that for many years beyond A.D. 2000 total water shortages for the U.S. as a whole are highly improbable.

If water is going to remain so plentiful into the 21st century, why should New York and other cities find themselves running short in 1965? The immediate answer, of course, is that there has been a five-year drought in the northeastern U.S. With the completion in 1955 of two new reservoirs in the upper reaches of the Delaware River, and with the extension of the Delaware aqueduct to a total distance of more than 120 miles, New York City believed it could satisfy its water needs until the year 2000. This confident forecast reckoned without the unprecedented drought.

There is no point in criticizing New York's decision to depend so heavily on the Delaware watershed for its future needs. The question is what New York should do now. As long ago as 1950, in an earlier water shortage, New York was advised to build a pumping station on the Hudson River 65 miles north of the city to provide an emergency supply of 100 million gallons per day, or more as needed. (New York City's normal water demand is about 1.2 b.g.d. The average flow of the Hudson is around 11 b.g.d.) The State of New York gave the city permission to build the pumping station but stipulated that the station be dismantled when the emergency was over. By the time the station was built (at a point somewhat farther south than the one recommended) the drought had ended; the station was torn down without ever having been used. In July 1965 the city asked the state for permission to rebuild the station, a job that will take several months, but as of mid-August permission had not been granted.

Meanwhile there has been much talk of building atomic-energy desalination plants as the long-term solution to New York's water needs. The economic justification for such proposals has never been explained. New York now obtains its water, delivered by gravity flow to the city, for only about 15 cents per 1,000 gallons (and many consumers are charged only 12 cents). The lowest predicted cost for desalination, assuming a plant with a capacity of 250 million or more gallons per day, is a highly optimistic 30 to 50 cents per 1,000 gallons. Since a desalination plant would be at sea level, its entire output would have to be pumped; storage and conveyance together would add about 20 cents per 1,000 gallons to the basic production cost. Recent studies in our department at Johns Hopkins University have shown that if desalinated water could be produced and delivered for as little as 50 cents per 1,000 gallons, it would still be cheaper to obtain fresh water from a supply 600 miles away. (The calculations assume a water demand of 100 million gallons per day.) In other words, it would be much cheaper for New York City to pipe water 270 miles from the St. Lawrence River, assuming that Canada gave its consent, than to build a desalination plant at the edge of town. New York City does not have to go even as far as the St. Lawrence. It has large untapped reserves in the Hudson River and in the upper watershed of the Susquehanna, no more than 150 miles away, that could meet the city's needs well beyond the year 2000.

Few cities in the U.S. have the range of alternatives open to New York. The great majority of inland cities draw their water supplies from the nearest lake or river. Of the more than 150 million Americans now served by public water supplies, nearly 100 million, or 60 percent, are reusing water from sources that have already been used at least once for domestic sewage and industrial waste disposal. This "used" water has of course been purified, either naturally or artificially, before it reaches the consumer. Only about 25 percent of the 25 b.g.d. now used by municipalities is obtained from aquifers, or underground sources. Such aquifers supply about 65 b.g.d. of the nation's estimated 1965 requirement of 370 b.g.d. Most of the 65 b.g.d. is merely a subterranean portion of the 1,200 b.g.d. of the precipitation flowing steadily to the sea. It is estimated, however, that from five to 10 b.g.d. is water "mined" from aquifers that have been filled over the centuries. Most of this mining is done in West Texas, New Mexico, Arizona and California.

The fact that more than 150 million Americans can be provided with safe drinking water by municipal waterworks, regardless of their source of supply, attests the effectiveness of modern water-treatment methods. Basically the treatment consists of filtration and chlorination. The use of chlorine to kill bacteria in municipal water supplies was introduced in 1908. It is fortunate that such a cheap and readily available substance is so effective. A typical requirement is about one part of chlorine to a million parts of water (one p.p.m.). The amount of chlorine needed to kill bacteria and also to "kill" the taste of dissolved organic substances—many of which are introduced naturally when rainwater comes in contact with decaying vegetation—is adjusted by monitoring the amount of free chlorine present in the water five to 10 minutes after treatment. This residual chlorine is usually held to about .2 p.p.m. In cases where unusually large amounts of organic compounds are present in the water, causing the public to complain of a bad taste, experience has shown that the palatability of the water can often be improved simply by adding more chlorine. Contrary to a widely held impression, free chlorine itself has little taste; the "bad" taste usually attributed to chlorine is due chiefly to organic compounds that have been too lightly chlorinated. When they are more heavily chlorinated, the bad taste usually disappears.

Throughout history impure water has been a leading cause of fatal disease in man; such waterborne diseases as typhoid fever and dysentery were still common in the U.S. less than a century ago. In 1900 the U.S. death rate from typhoid fever was 35.8 per 100,000 people. If such a rate persisted today, the deaths from typhoid would far exceed those from automobile accidents. By

1936 the rate had been reduced to 2.5 per 100,000, and today the disease is almost unknown in the U.S.

In underdeveloped nations, where many cities are still without adequate water supplies, waterborne diseases are among the leading causes of death and debility. In Central and South America more than a third of 75 million people living in towns or cities with a population of more than 2,000 are without water service. Similarly, in India about a third of the urban population of 80 million are without an adequate water supply. As the chapter on Calcutta in this book [page 59] points out, that city is regarded as the endemic center of cholera for all of southeast Asia.

No general prescription can be offered for bringing clean water to the vast urban populations that still lack it. I have found in my own experience, however, that the inhabitants of communities both large and small can do much more to help themselves than is customarily recognized. If the small towns and villages of India and elsewhere wait for their central governments to install public water supplies, most of them will wait indefinitely. It is surprising how much can be accomplished with local labor and local materials, and the benefits in health are incalculable.

In the larger cities, where self-help is not feasible, municipal water systems can be built and made to pay their way if an appropriate charge is made for water and if the systems can be financed with long-term loans, as they have been financed traditionally in the U.S. Such loans, however, have only recently been made available to underdeveloped countries. A few years ago, when loans for waterworks had to be paid off in six to 12 years, the total value of external bank loans made to South American countries for water supply and sewerage projects was less than $100,000 in a six-year period. Under the leadership of the Pan-American Health Organization and the U.S. Agency for International Development bankers were encouraged to extend the repayment period to 28 or 30 years. Today the total value of bank loans made to South American countries for waterworks and sewerage systems has surpassed $660 million.

Outside the U.S., as within it, adequate water resources are generally available. The problem is to treat water as a commodity whose cost to the user must bear a fair relation to the cost of its production and delivery. The total U.S. investment in municipal waterworks is about $17.5 billion (replacement cost would approach $50 billion), or about half the nation's investment in telephone service. More significant than investment is the cost of service to the consumer. The average American family pays about $3 a month for water, which it cannot live without, compared with about $7.30 for telephone service. One might also note that the average household expenditure for alcoholic beverages is more than $15 a month. It should be clear that Americans can afford to pay for all the water they need.

The question of fair payment and allocation of costs is even more central to the problem of controlling water pollution than to the problem of providing water. Whereas 150 million Americans were served by waterworks in 1963, only about 120 million were served by sewers. Thus the wastes of nearly 70 million Americans, who live chiefly in the smaller towns and suburbs, were still being piped into backyard cesspools and septic tanks. When these devices are properly designed and the receiving soils are not overloaded, they create no particular sanitation hazard. Unfortunately in too many suburban areas neither of these criteria is met.

The principal pollution hazard arises where sewage collected by a sewerage system is discharged into a lake or river without adequate treatment or without any treatment at all. As of 1962 the wastes of nearly 15 million Americans were discharged untreated and the wastes of 2.4 million received only minor treatment. The wastes of 32.7 million were given primary treatment: passage through a settling basin, which removes a considerable portion of the suspended solid matter. Intermediate treatment, which consists of a more nearly complete removal of solids, was applied to the wastes of 7.4 million people. Secondary treatment, the most adequate form of sewage treatment, was applied to the wastes of 61.2 million people. The term "secondary treatment" covers a variety of techniques, often used in combination: extended aeration, activated sludge (an accelerated form of bacterial degradation), filtration through beds of various materials, stabilization ponds.

Although there was a significant improvement in sewage treatment in the U.S. between 1942 and 1962, a big job remains to be done. Only in the past five years of this period did the rate of sewer installation begin to overtake population growth. The present U.S. investment in sewers and sewage-treatment works is about $12 billion (again the replacement value would be much higher). The Public Health Service estimates that replacing obsolete facilities, improving the standard of treatment and providing for population growth will require an annual investment of more than $800 million a year in treatment works for the rest of the decade. This does not include the cost of extending the sewage-collection systems into new urban and suburban developments. This may add another $800 million to the annual requirements, making an approximate total of more than $1.6 billion a year.

Unfortunately some municipalities have not found a satisfactory or painless method for charging their residents for this vital service. Many simply float bonds to meet capital costs and add the cost to the individual's bill for property taxes. In Baltimore (where the tax bill is completely itemized) it was decided some years ago that sewerage costs should not be included in the citizen's *ad valorem* taxes but should be made part of his water bill. In the Baltimore system the charge for sewerage service is half the water service charge. A good many other cities charge for sewerage service on a similar basis.

Cities, of course, account for only a part, and probably not the major part, of the pollution that affects the nation's waterways. Industrial pollution is a ubiquitous problem. Industrial pollutants are far more varied than those in ordinary sewage, and their removal often calls for specialized measures. Even in states where adequate pollution-control laws are on the books, there are technological, economic and practical obstacles to seeing that the laws are observed. The Federal Water Pollution Control acts of 1954 and 1962, which enlarged the role of the Public Health Service in determining the pollution of interstate waterways, have sometimes been helpful in strengthening the hand of local law-enforcement agencies.

My final topic—air pollution—is much harder to discuss in quantitative terms than water pollution, which it otherwise resembles in many ways. It is never going to be possible to provide a collection system for air pollution emissions, almost all of which result from combustion processes. Every house, every apartment, every automobile, truck, bus, factory and power plant is vented directly into the open air and presumably will have to remain so.

There are perhaps only three general approaches to controlling the amount of pollutants entering the atmosphere. One is to switch from a fuel that produces undesirable combustion products to one that produces fewer such products. Thus fuel oil produces less soot and fly ash than bituminous coal, and natural gas produces less than either. The second expedient is to employ a new technology. For example, atomic power plants produce none of the particulate and gaseous emissions that result from the burning of fossil fuels. One must then decide, however, whether the radioactive by-products that are released into the environment—either in the short run or the long—by an atomic power station are more or less hazardous than the fossil-fuel by-products they replaced. The third recourse is to remove the undesired components from the vented gases. Fly ash, for example, can be largely removed by suitable devices where coal or oil is used in large volume, as in a power plant, but cannot readily be removed from the flue gases of thousands of residences. The problem of dealing with many small offending units also arises in trying to reduce the unburned hydrocarbons and carbon monoxide emitted by millions of automobiles.

At this point it is worth asking: Why should air pollution be considered objectionable? Many people enjoy the smell of the pollutants released by a steak sizzling on a charcoal grill or by dry leaves burning in the fall. The cigarette smoker obviously enjoys the smoke he draws into his lungs. In other words, a pollutant per se need not necessarily be regarded as a nuisance. If by accident or design the exhaust gases emitted by a diesel bus had a fragrant aroma (or worse yet, led to physiological addiction), not many people would complain about traffic fumes.

The criteria of what constitutes an objectionable air pollutant must therefore be subjectively defined, unless, of course, one can demonstrate that a particular pollutant is a hazard to health. In the absence of a demonstrated health hazard the city dweller would probably list his complaints somewhat as follows: he objects to soot and dirt, he does not want his eyes to burn and water, he dislikes traffic fumes and he wishes he could see the clear blue sky more often.

Many conferences have been held and many papers written on the possible association of air pollution with disease. As might be expected, firm evidence of harmfulness is difficult to obtain. The extensive epidemiological data collected in the U.S. on smoking and human health suggest that in general place of residence has a minor influence on the incidence of lung cancer compared with the smoking habit itself. British statistics, however, can be interpreted to show that at times there is something harmful in the British air. In any event, it will be difficult to demonstrate conclusively—no matter how much one may believe it to be so—that air pollution is associated with long-term deterioration of the human organism. Eric J. Cassell of the Cornell University Medical College recently summarized the situation as follows: "I do not think that it is wrong to say that we do not even know what disease or diseases are caused by everyday pollution of our urban air. . . . We have a cause, but no disease to go with it."

Two diseases frequently mentioned as possibly associated with air pollution are chronic bronchitis and pulmonary emphysema. In Britain some investigators have found strong associations between chronic bronchitis and the level of air pollution, as measured by such indexes as fuel use, sulfur dioxide in the air and sootfall. In California the death rate from emphysema increased fourfold in the seven-year period from 1950 to 1957. This increase may indicate nothing more than the fact that older people go to California to retire, but there is objective evidence that emphysematous patients in Los Angeles showed improved lung function when allowed to breathe carefully filtered air for 48 hours.

In response to mounting public concern, and the urging of President Johnson, Congress in 1963 passed the Clean Air Act, which states in its preamble that "Federal financial assistance and leadership is essential for the development of cooperative Federal, state, regional and local programs designed to prevent and control air polution." The regulatory abatement procedures authorized in the act are similar to those found in the most recent Water Pollution Control Act. When an interstate pollution problem is identified, the Public Health Service is empowered, as a first step, to call a conference of state and local agencies. The second step is to call a public hearing, and the third step, if needed, is to bring a court action against the offenders.

The Clean Air Act takes special cognizance of air pollution caused by motor vehicles; it requires the Secretary of Health,

Education, and Welfare to report periodically to Congress on progress made on control devices. He is also invited to recommend any new legislation he feels is warranted. Eventually the Secretary may help to decide if all new U.S. motor vehicles should be equipped with exhaust-control systems, such as "afterburners," to reduce the large amounts of unburned hydrocarbons and carbon monoxide that are now released.

California studies in the 1950's showed that exhaust gases accounted for 65 percent of all the unburned hydrocarbons then produced by motor vehicles. Another 15 percent represented evaporation from the fuel tank and carburetor, and 20 percent escaped from the vent of the crankcase. As a first step in reducing these emissions California began in 1961 to require the use of crankcase blowby devices, which became standard on all U.S. cars beginning with the 1963 models.

A new California law will require exhaust-control systems on all 1966 automobiles and light trucks sold in the state. The law is intended to reduce by 70 or 80 percent the amount of hydrocarbons now present in exhaust gases and to reduce the carbon monoxide by 60 percent. All the carbon monoxide is generated by combustion and is now released in the exhaust. From 1940 to 1965 there has been a steady rise in carbon monoxide vented into the atmosphere of Los Angeles County.

No one questions that an affluent society can afford to spend its money without a strict accounting of benefits received. Any reasonable expenditure that promises to improve the quality of life in the modern city should be welcomed. It is not obvious, however, that any American city except Los Angeles will be significantly benefited by the installation of exhaust-control systems in motor vehicles. The cost of these systems will not be trivial. At an estimated $40 to $50 per car, such systems would add more than $300 million to the sales price of new cars in an eight-million-car year—and this does not include the annual cost of their inspection and maintenance. If one objective of reducing the air pollution caused by automobiles is to increase the life expectancy of the city dweller, or simply to make his life more pleasant, it can be argued that $300 million a year could be spent more usefully in other directions.

In most large cities, for example, the electric utilities consume up to half of all fuel burned. Most utilities have made reasonable efforts to reduce the emission of soot and fly ash; virtually all new power plants, and many old ones, are now equipped with devices capable of removing a large fraction of such emissions. Utilities, however, are still under pressure, both from the public and from supervising agencies, to use the cheapest fuels available. This means that in New York and other eastern-seaboard cities the utilities burn large volumes of residual fuel oil imported from abroad, which happens to contain between 2.5 and 3 percent of sulfur, compared with only about 1.7 percent for domestic fuel oil. When the oil is burned, sulfur dioxide is released. Recent studies show that the level of sulfur dioxide in New York City air is almost twice that found in other large cities.

Sulfur dioxide is difficult to remove from stack gases, but it is estimated that for about $1 a barrel most of the sulfur could be removed from the oil before it is burned. For the volume of oil burned by the Consolidated Edison Company in New York City the added cost would come to about $15 million annually. If the cost were divided among Consolidated Edison's three million customers, the average electric bill would be increased about $5 per year. One would like to know how this expenditure would compare in improving the quality of New York City's air with New York's pro rata share of the more than $300-million-a-year investment that would be required by the installation of exhaust-control systems in motor vehicles. That share would be on the order of $8 million a year. Perhaps New Yorkers should insist on both investments. But these are only two of many options, all of them expensive. It is the responsibility of the city administrator and the public health officer to make choices and assign priorities, even while admitting that air pollution is never beneficial.

One must also recall that when large-scale changes are contemplated, the whole spectrum of society is involved. Rarely do all forces march forward in step, particularly where public policy and scientific verity are not crystal clear. Competitive forces delay correctives until public opinion rises in wrath and pushes for action on an *ad hoc* and intuitive basis.

Let me sum up by observing that in the case of water supply the accomplishments of the U.S. have been extraordinarily good, not only in the prevention of waterborne and water-associated diseases but also in providing water generously for comfortable living in most places at most times. The prospect for the future is likewise good. The realities are that we are not running out of water and that we are capable of managing our water resources intelligently.

In the area of water and air pollution our successes are only partial. Rapid urbanization and industrialization have intensified the problems of controlling both. At the same time one must concede that there is much stronger scientific justification for mounting vigorous programs to abate water pollution than to abate air pollution. Nevertheless, public pressure on behalf of the latter is increasing, and as has happened so often in the past, we may find action running ahead of knowledge. This is not necessarily to be deplored.

My own view coincides with that recently expressed by P. B. Medawar of University College London at a symposium on the interaction of man and his environment. "We are not yet qualified," he said, "to prescribe for the medical welfare of our grandchildren. . . . I should say that present skills are sufficient for present ills."

The Renewal of Cities

· NATHAN GLAZER

Many U.S. cities, with the aid of the Federal Government, are engaged in ambitious efforts to renew themselves. It is not certain, however, that the overall gains of these programs have outweighed the losses.

WHEN WE SPEAK of the renewal of cities, we mean all the processes whereby cities are maintained or rebuilt: the replacement of old houses by new houses, of older streets by newer streets, the transformation of commercial areas, the relocation of industrial facilities, the rebuilding of public utilities; we refer to rehabilitation as well as demolition and rebuilding; we mean too the laws and administrative and financial mechanisms by which this rebuilding and rehabilitation are accomplished. The only way to discuss such an enormous subject is to consider all the elements of change in a city: its changing economic role, its changing population, decisions to buy or sell, stay or move, rehabilitate or demolish, and the larger market and political forces that affect all this.

Fortunately we can narrow our subject considerably. There exist, in this nation and others, specific public policies designed to plan and control at least some part of these vast processes. In the U.S. such policies are expressed in the urban renewal program administered by the Urban Renewal Administration (a part of the Federal Housing and Home Finance Agency), which guides hundreds of local city agencies in the effort to transform urban renewal from a process dominated by the requirements and opportunities of the market to one guided by social intelligence—reflection on how the process might best create a better city.

The specific program that is the focus of this chapter began with the passage of the Housing Act of 1949 and has been expanded and modified continually since then. Before that time, of course, there were many mechanisms by which cities and states and the Federal Government attempted to affect the rebuilding of cities. The most significant Federal predecessor of urban renewal was public housing, that is, slum clearance and the building of subsidized Government housing for the poor. There remains a good deal of confusion between public housing and urban renewal. Indeed, the agency that is responsible for New York City's huge program of urban renewal, the largest in the nation, was until a few years ago called the Slum Clearance Commission. A similar agency in Chicago was called the Land Clearance Commission. And under the original Housing Act the effort to guide urban renewal was administered by a Division of Slums and Urban Redevelopment. All these agencies now have different names that foretell the sparkling new structures that will go on cleared land rather than the grimy ones that are to be cleared. Therein lies one of the great dilemmas of our approach to urban renewal: the fact that our program provides great powers and resources for clearing the way to get new areas built but few resources for dealing with the people who live in the older areas that are to be cleared.

Federally supported public housing was only one of the ways in which government had tried to deal with urban problems before the development of a comprehensive renewal program. There were also Federally sponsored mortgage-insurance programs that helped to make possible the widespread construction of private, single-family houses in the suburbs of U.S. cities after World War II. In addition there were numerous efforts on the part of cities to control development and redevelopment with zoning regulations, health and building regulations concerning housing, and the establishment of local planning agencies. The urban renewal program made use of these local powers of planning and zoning, Federal credit mechanisms and the existing power to clear slums and build public housing; it added to these older approaches a powerful legal mechanism and a powerful financial mechanism, both designed to win the cooperation of private developers in the pursuit of public goals. The legal mechanism stipulated that a local renewal agency was empowered to condemn private property not only for public uses (which had long been permitted) and publicly owned housing but also for resale to private developers who agreed to fulfill the plan for the area that the local agency had drawn up. The financial mechanism, known as a write-down, committed the Federal Government to paying from two-thirds to three-quarters of the difference between, on the one hand, the cost of buying the land, clearing it and preparing it for the new development and, on the other, the price that private redevelopers would pay for it. The designers of the urban renewal legislation were proposing a compromise: public intelligence was to guide the rebuilding of cities, but the rebuilding would be carried out in such a way as to ensure significant private profits and ultimate private ownership of land the public had spent a great deal of money and effort to acquire.

The power of condemnation assured private developers that they could acquire large tracts. These were sought because they prevent the remaining slums from pressing too close on the renewed area, diminishing its desirability, value and profit for the owner. One social critic, Jane Jacobs, has dramatically questioned the need for such large tracts in her book *The Death and Life of Great American Cities*. Most modern planners, however, tend to endorse the developers' demand for large areas, citing the need for more parking and park space. As for the financial write-down, private developers sought it because the price of central-city slum areas was high, even if one took away from the property owners the right to raise their prices excessively. The slums were densely occupied and lucrative for the landlords, favorably located and well served by public transportation and city facilities. In certain areas the financial power to write down the cost of land became far more important than the power to condemn. In Manhattan, for example, the redevelopment of urban renewal property has cost the public $1 million an acre—the difference between what was paid the owners of the land in order to clear it and what the developers paid to have the opportunity to redevelop it. In other areas developers were quite willing to pay the condemnation cost of the land, and it was the power to condemn and assemble that made redevelopment possible.

We have described the mechanisms of urban renewal; what were the objectives of the program? These can be ascertained if we examine the disparate elements in the alliance that forged it. There were first of all people committed to public planning and public housing. In 1949 these were the men and women who had participated in the great experiments of the New Deal, in which a modicum of European social imagination and concern in the area of housing had been introduced into the U.S. They saw urban renewal—even if they had qualms about the compromise embodied in the legislation—as a means of extending the power of the people to affect through politics the growth of their cities and the quality of their housing and environment, thus reducing the power of the market to shape this for them. Tied to the original urban renewal legislation was provision for a good deal of public housing that would foreseeably accommodate those who had to be relocated from the demolished slums. It was unpleasant from the point of view of the reformers to have to pay the owners of slum property so much money for the privilege of replanning and rebuilding the areas, but the alternatives had been vetoed. One such alternative, put forward by Charles Abrams and Catherine Bauer Wurster, called for building more public housing on open and cheap land on the outskirts of a city and allowing the price of central slum properties to fall as they emptied. Such a solution was opposed by the big-city mayors and the commercial and financial interests dependent on maintaining business and property values in the centers of the big cities—in particular, department store owners and banks with mortgages on central-city property.

Urban renewal was created by an alliance of those seeking reform and those seeking profit. The planners and advocates of public housing were trying to improve the environment of slum dwellers and the overall pattern of the city in terms of amenity and efficiency. The commercial and financial interests were trying to maintain the level of business and property values in downtown areas, jeopardized somewhat by an increasingly poor (and, incidentally, nonwhite) central-city populace. Both groups wanted to stem the rapid flow of the more prosperous citizens to the suburbs and hoped this could be done by remodeling the cities physically. The mayors, confronted with the increasing costs of urban government and threatened by the decline of property values and tax revenues, shared this hope. They saw in urban renewal the solution to the economic decline of central-city areas and an opportunity to build monuments and generally beautify the cities.

The alliance is no longer intact. The downtown commercial interests still support the program. The mayors still support it, seeing no alternative. The planners are split. Those who emphasize the social aims of planning, the problems of the poor and the slum dwellers, oppose the program on the grounds that it has done little for the poor and nothing to reverse the pattern of increased urban segregation. These planners are torn between their commitment to the ideal of the people shaping their own environment and their dismay at the actual environment that, under political and economic pressure, has been shaped. Most planners, however, support urban renewal; for one thing, the planners of today are not the planners of the 1940's who participated in the New Deal or whose ideas were molded by it. They are now in large part the professionals trained to fill needs created by the urban renewal program itself.

Let us review the present state of the program, taking our information from the report of the Housing and Home Finance Agency for 1964. By the end of that year local renewal agencies had acquired about 27,000 acres of urban land. "Redevelopers had been selected for 16,318 acres"; the rest was being cleared or was unsold. "Redevelopment had been completed or was actually under construction on more than 55 percent of that land," or about one-third of all the land that had been acquired. "By mid-1964, more than 72 percent of all land disposed of, exclusive of streets and alleys, had been purchased by private persons or organizations. More than half was intended for residential purposes. By mid-1964, 61,770 dwelling units of all kinds were completed and 18,300 more were under construction"—some 80,000 in all. The sum of Federal money involved in this effort—the capital grants that would eventually be required to complete this volume of urban renewal—was $4.3 billion. Midway through 1964 some 176,000 families and 74,000 individuals had been relocated from sites scheduled for urban renewal.

The scale of this undertaking seems different from various perspectives. Bernard Frieden, professor of city planning at the Massachusetts Institute of Technology and former editor of the *Journal of the American Institute of Planners*, estimates that deteriorated housing in New York City in 1960 covered 1,145 acres. The number of units of deteriorated housing recorded by the census of 1960 was 147,000. This suggests that the urban renewal program was of a sufficient order of magnitude to clear away all the slums of New York—if all of the program had been devoted to that city (and if it had been used to clear away slums, and if there had been policies to prevent new slums from forming). On the other hand, the 80,000 units of housing built or under construction since the beginning of urban renewal in 1949 is not an impressive total compared with the 7.3 million housing units built between 1960 and 1964, nor does the relocation of some 750,000 people seem highly significant in view of the fact that 40 million people move every year in the U.S.

Obviously one can say that renewal has just begun to scratch the surface of the need; there were, after all, 2.3 million substandard dwellings in our cities in 1960. It is also being said, however, that renewal has already gone too far, or at least too far in the wrong direction. Social critics allege that although the volume of building under the urban renewal program has been slight, its impact on certain parts of the population has been devastating. In some cities the designation for urban renewal of any area, no matter how decrepit the housing, arouses a desperate resistance among the people living there. Indeed, television dramas of daily life sometimes cast the local urban renewal agency in the role once played by the hardhearted banker. This adverse reputation, a powerful comment on urban renewal, seems to arise from the real experience of the poor; it was not created by the social critics who now amplify it. The urban renewal agency does in fact represent a current threat to many: destroying small businessmen, evicting older people from their homes, forcing families from their tenements and then failing to relocate them in decent, safe, sanitary and reasonably priced housing as required by law, threat-

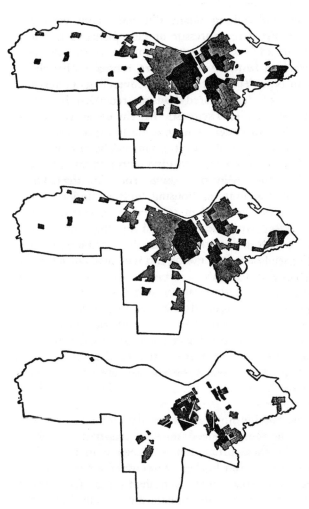

IMPACT OF RENEWAL ON NEGROES AND POOR is suggested by three maps of Philadelphia. Maps at left and right are based on 1960 census data. Map at left shows tracts where nonwhite population exceeded 80 percent (black) and tracts where it was 50 to 80 percent (gray). Map at right shows tracts where average family income was less than $4,720 annually (black) and where it fell between $4,720 and $6,000 (gray). Map in center shows zones scheduled for renewal by reconstruction (black) or renovation (gray). Dislocation of Negroes and the poor has been minimized in Philadelphia, but the problem is a continuing one in national program.

ening buildings of historic or architectural value, and even attack-
ing Bohemians and artists in their contemporary garrets. (These
are the most dangerous opponents, because they know how to get
publicity.) It is apparent that the urban renewal agency is a more
vivid threat to security than the banker in these days of amortized
mortgages.

Still, if the scale of urban renewal has been as small as I have indicated in terms of figures for voluntary movement of population,
new dwellings built and people directly affected, how is it possible to argue that its effects on the city have been so damaging?
Primarily because its impact has been on one segment of the urban
population: the poor—those least able, materially or psycho-
logically, to adapt to upheaval. The people who live in old neighborhoods are, compared with the rest of the U.S. population,
poor, old and more likely to be Negroes or members of other
minority groups. They are often people with special ties to the
neighborhood and special problems that keep them there. For
many reasons, of which money is only one, they find it extremely
difficult to find other housing in the city. Two-thirds of those relocated from urban renewal sites have been non-whites (the program has sometimes been derisively termed "Negro removal"),
whose problem of finding housing is compounded by the fact that
few parts of the city will accept them. Many of the businesses on
urban renewal sites were small and marginal; indeed, some provided for an aged couple a living no better than what they would
get on welfare. Such people were nonetheless kept occupied, and
they provided some of the social benefits of an old neighborhood
that Jane Jacobs has described: places to leave messages, conver-
sation to break the monotony and anonymity of city living, eyes
to watch the street. Some 39,000 business properties had been
acquired by urban renewal agencies as of September 30, 1963;
studies have shown that a third do not survive relocation. Some of
them would have succumbed to the high death rate of small businesses in any case. Many that do relocate successfully move outside the city; thus ironically the city loses the taxes from business
that urban renewal is meant to increase.

The urban renewal agency is required to demonstrate that
enough housing is available for those whose homes are to be
demolished, it is required to help them move and it has Federal

resources to pay moving expenses for families and businesses. These requirements were much looser at the beginning of the urban renewal program than they are today, and the resources available were much scantier. Among the first large urban renewal projects in Manhattan were those undertaken by the energetic Robert Moses at a time when New York had a great shortage of housing, particularly low-cost housing. Relocation was unquestionably carried out in a businesslike and ruthless fashion (that is, rapidly on those sites where the developers were eager to move out the people and put up the new buildings, slowly on sites where they preferred to collect rents from the slum dwellers they were supposed to evict). Available aid, in the form of money or advice or social service, was slight. The image of renewal, as of many things in this country, is largely set by what happens in New York, where most of the writers, publishers and television producers live; urban renewal began with a very poor image. It is uncertain whether enough has been done to correct the practices that created the nightmare one critic calls "the Federal bulldozer."

According to reports sent to Washington from local authorities, the dwellings of 87 percent of the families relocated from urban renewal sites are known and were inspected, and 92 percent of these are decent, safe and sanitary as required by law. These figures have been disputed by Chester Hartman, a city planner who worked on a major study of the impact of urban renewal conducted by the Center for Community Studies in Boston. Hartman argues that local authorities have loose standards in judging the quality of the housing into which people move from urban renewal sites. Thus the local agency reported that less than 2 percent of the families relocated from Boston's West End had moved into structurally substandard housing, whereas the Center for Community Studies placed the figure at 25 percent. Conversely, the local authorities tend to apply strict standards in judging the housing of an area they plan to demolish, because they have to satisfy Washington that the area is a genuine slum. Herbert Gans (in *The Urban Villagers*, a detailed description of the West End as an old, inner-city working-class district) has pointed out that what was a slum to the planners was good housing to those who lived there—housing they preferred to any other in the city, and in a neighborhood that contained the people and places they knew.

The West End study demonstrated that there was an improvement in the quality of the housing into which most families were relocated and an increase in the proportion of home owners. There was also an increase in rents: the median rent of the West Enders rose from $41 to $71 a month, and rent as a proportion of income rose from 14 to 19 percent. Similar studies have been completed in recent years, some of which indicate that before renewal the West End was a real bargain. Although the figures vary from survey to survey, the results of relocation form a pattern: housing is somewhat improved, rents go up, the proportion of rent to income goes up, home ownership increases.

How are we to evaluate such a pattern? There is currently great interest among city planners and urban economists in developing a technique for quantitative comparison of costs and benefits, a technique that could in every case give an objective answer to the question: Is this urban renewal project worth it? Attempts at cost-benefit analysis have in the past been crude. For example, planners have compared the costs of police, welfare and other social services of an area to be leveled with the reduced costs after rebuilding, neglecting to take into account the fact that the costs are incurred not by neighborhoods or buildings but by people. The departure of the people does not, of course, reduce the costs; it merely changes the place where the costs are incurred. As Martin Anderson has shown in his critique of urban renewal, *The Federal Bulldozer*, even the simple analysis of tax returns from the property before and after redevelopment is often inadequate, since it may fail to take into account such elements as the loss of taxes during the long period of redevelopment and the possibility that the same new structures might have been built elsewhere in the city without redevelopment.

If the tangible aspects of renewal are difficult to evaluate in the balance sheet of a cost-benefit analysis, how can one assess such intangibles as the cost of relocating an old woman whose only remaining satisfactions in life are taking care of the apartment in which she has lived for many years, going to the church around the corner and exchanging a few words with the neighborhood merchants? Admittedly one can even work in these costs by reckoning the chance that she will require a nursing home when she moves, or some additional city service. Such tabulations may at times seem akin to dissecting a rainbow, but they are being made nonetheless. The major purpose of the West End study has been to determine the impact of relocation on the mental health of the participants. Reports by Marc Fried of the Harvard Medical School indicate that serious reactions of grief have exceeded, in depth and duration, most expectations.

Even if we can find a way of quantifying the intangible aspects of relocation, how are we to take them into account in making social policy? The decisions to renew or not to renew must be made by local governments responsive to the pressures of the different parts of the community. If the political costs of a certain course of action are great, they will certainly outweigh the results of any subtle analysis of psychological, social and economic costs or benefits. Experience so far shows that almost invariably the despair in areas slated for demolition is not channeled into meaningful political opposition; it is outweighed by the arguments for renewal presented by planners to the city fathers and the prejudice among middle-class citizens against allowing what they consider slums to remain standing near them. The proponents of renewal have not, however, been oblivious to its reputation among the poor; with each subsequent housing act they have expanded the resources for relocating families and have heightened the obligation of local authorities to do the same. Let us review briefly the resources now available to the local urban renewal agency for dealing with this problem.

Families on sites scheduled for demolition have always had priority in moving into public housing. The amount of public housing built has approximated the amount demolished. In general, however, only half the families on a site are eligible for public housing, and all told only 20 percent of the relocated families have moved into it. Often there is not enough public housing available at the precise time it is needed. The local public housing authority and the local renewal authority are two separate bodies; they deal with two separate agencies in Washington; they operate under separate laws, and although specific public housing projects theoretically could be built in anticipation of an old neighborhood being cleared, this has not often been done. In any case, many of those eligible for public housing will not accept it; this is particularly true of white families, who often refuse to move into projects in which they feel the proportion of Negroes is too high. Negroes and whites alike object to the institutional atmosphere of projects, with their regulations and requirements, and all share the apprehension that public housing attracts a concentration of problem families.

Since 1954 one of the major objectives of urban renewal has been the rehabilitation of old houses—a process that makes relocation unnecessary. Unfortunately rehabilitation, even with Federal loan programs to promote it, has rarely been successful. Renovating a house to meet the standards imposed by the program requires much more money than the occupants can raise; the property is then sold to a new owner. The general result is that poor people are moved out of houses that upper-income people can afford to renovate.

The sums available for relocating families and businesses were originally small, and they were provided only when they were needed to expedite development. These sums have been increased sharply and are now given more readily. The 1964 Housing Act for the first time recognizes and authorizes payment (of up to $500) to families, elderly individuals and small businessmen for the dislocations attendant on moving. It has taken 15 years for this principle, which is taken for granted in other countries, to be recognized by our government. Late but useful aid has also been extended by the Small Business Administration, which was authorized in 1961 to help businessmen reestablish themselves with loans, assistance and information.

Still other efforts have been made to ease the burdens of relocation. In the early 1950's special loans were designed to provide housing for those from urban renewal sites who were too poor to get regular housing but not poor enough to be eligible for public housing. The most successful type of loan was instituted in 1961; it permits nonprofit sponsors as well as limited-dividend corporations to get mortgages below the going rate to put up cooperative or rental housing for moderate-income families. There has also been a strengthening of Federal regulations requiring detailed reports from local agencies on the availability of housing (in different price ranges and for nonwhites as well as whites), on relocation plans and on current progress. Finally, the explosion of new social welfare programs for the poor provides additional resources. On the West Side of Manhattan, where extensive relocation is under way, a substantial number of social workers are engaged in various programs to help families find housing and settle in a new environment.

Gradually, after 15 years of putting so much energy into getting buildings down and so little into helping people up, we are beginning to develop the kind of program that should have existed from the beginning and that exists in the advanced European welfare state—a program whose emphasis is on providing housing. We are still faced by immense problems of segregation, institutionalism in public housing and human uprooting, but as of 1965 it should be possible for most local urban renewal authorities to carry out an effective relocation plan and even provide some of those benefits from relocation that the advocates of urban renewal maintain the process makes possible.

The question now becomes: What positive goals are we attempting to attain through renewal? How well does the renewal program make it possible to achieve them? It is not enough to say that we want new buildings instead of old buildings. Urban economists argue that in any event buildings will go up in response to market demands; urban renewal has merely shifted the location of new buildings rather than increased their actual number. Unquestionably renewal has done a good deal to bring investment into downtown areas, but what has the public gained by investing hundreds of millions of dollars for new street layouts, parking, open space and land write-downs for private developers—all for shoring up the center of the city? The answer is usually stated in terms of tradition or economics: The center must remain strong if a metropolitan area is to thrive. It must have good commercial and cultural facilities, and a significant proportion of middle- and upper-income residents. If private, unguided investment insists on going to the outlying suburbs (a tendency encouraged by the automobile, freeways and cheap suburban land), then public investment must redress the balance. Only in this way can the central city retain the middle- and upper-income people whose tax revenues enable it to provide services.

Both aspects of the defense of the central city have been chal-

lenged. Scott Greer of Northwestern University and Melvin
Webber of the University of California at Berkeley observe that
the form of the city is changing in such a way that Los Angeles
will be the most likely model of the city of the future. They hold
that behind the abandonment of the traditional city form is the
fact that free citizens in an affluent society—particularly those
with children—prefer to live in detached houses with some land.
This seems to be true the world over; it is only where costs make
such an arrangement impossible that people settle for apartment
houses. To rebuild expensive inner-city land for residential purposes means building apartments, attractive only to such special
elements as those without children—the young or the old. Certainly these groups represent an important market, but it does
not follow that government should provide them with a subsidy.
As for the economic argument—the need to attract the wealthy—
it has been attacked as a form of discrimination against the poor.
After all, the poor have come to the city's center because housing
there is cheapest and most convenient for them. They are near
their jobs, their friends and, in the case of immigrants, their families or countrymen. If the cities need subsidies to counter the increase in low-income residents, why must the subsidy take the
form of urban renewal? Why not redistribute Federal taxes to
cities on the basis of need and let the city choose how to spend it?
If we do this, a city made up largely of low-income people need
not be a disaster.

   A more basic challenge can be made to the argument that we
need inner-city renewal to save the traditional centers. Why must
we accept the present boundaries of cities as being permanent?
These boundaries have been set by a variety of political accidents;
as a result where one city (Boston, for example) may be a small
part of a metropolitan area, another (Dallas) may embrace almost
an entire metropolitan region. If the boundaries of each city
could be redrawn to include most of the metropolitan area, the
wealthy, who had abandoned the center for the outskirts, would
again pay taxes to the city and the need for public investment in
the center would be reduced. There are still other reasons why
there should be some form of metropolitan government. Many
problems in the provision of services could be solved more easily

and effectively if they were examined from a metropolitan point of view rather than from the point of view of separate political entities within the metropolitan area [see "New York: A Metropolitan Region," by Benjamin Chinitz, page 105]. This is preeminently true of transportation, water supply, open space for recreation and air pollution. It seems inordinately difficult to reorganize metropolitan governments in this country rationally; we can only envy the relative ease with which the government of London has been reorganized by an act of Parliament. The U.S. Government encourages metropolitan planning, but it can do little to create metropolitan governments to supplant the disparate governments within a metropolitan region.

One of the real virtues of urban renewal is that it has induced local communities to consider their needs and plan to meet them. In 1954 the Federal Government required that each city entering into an urban renewal program develop all the major operations of city government necessary to guide the rebuilding of the city and to submit a "workable program"—proper building codes and zoning ordinances, a comprehensive city plan, an administrative organization that could fulfill it, proof of interested citizens and the like. By 1959 the U.S. had instituted the Community Renewal Program, which provides substantial sums of money to cities to project their future development needs and policies. This program has supported much sophisticated work involving simulation on computers of future urban development under alternative policies. Unfortunately too much of the current research and projection, no matter how imaginative, is oriented to the wrong scale: the city rather than the metropolitan area. Moreover, the major tool of the urban renewal program remains the specific project. It is still hoped that a better city can be achieved by supporting, by means of advantageous condemnation and land write-downs, specific projects based on the capacity to attract specific investment. This gives urban renewal an inherently spotty character.

Suppose it is—as I believe—essential that cities radically improve their function in inspecting buildings, requiring repairs and supporting them where necessary. Suppose a major way to improve. a city is to root out substandard buildings wherever they are rather than demolish a huge area that is decrepit in spots. What

Federal aid would be available for that? Much less than is available for the specific-project approach. Let me give an example.

A proposed project in San Francisco was going to cost $40 million. For this amount some 15,000 people would be relocated, their homes demolished and the land turned over, somewhat improved by new streets, to builders. This is an enormous expense for a city the size of San Francisco, the total annual budget of which is only about $350 million. The money, however, was to come from the Federal Government and from the point of view of the city the undertaking was free. This would not be the case if San Francisco chose an alternative project, such as a major program of code enforcement, demolition of substandard housing or loans for rehabilitation. Urban renewal law and practice indicate that only a small fraction of $40 million would be extended for such efforts.

All the criticisms of urban renewal point to the fact that, whereas the program speaks of the whole city and all the ways in which it must be improved, provisions are made to influence only one aspect of the city—the physical nature of a given locale. The program as constituted and as practiced makes too little use of the traditional agencies of city government that must be depended on to improve cities. It also relates poorly to other large programs and expenditures in the city, such as the freeway program. When we consider the imaginative urban renewal that has been carried out in some European and Japanese cities by closely linking transportation arteries, housing, commercial and office facilities, we wonder why our projects are so often massive concentrations of a single function: all housing here, all concert halls there, all shopping there—and all poorly linked by transportation. This is the logical result, I would argue, of the fact that our urban renewal authority in Washington and the local agencies are oriented toward single missions—and the mission in every case is the individual project rather than the whole city.

After some 16 years of urban renewal we are still struggling with the problem of slums and still trying to formulate some alternative to the naïve image of the city beautiful in its middle-class version, an image that has increasingly lost its power to move people and solve problems. Under the pressure of a number of gifted critics, urban renewal has become an instrument that any city can use to develop policies well suited to its needs, and to carry out some of them. It is by no means a perfect instrument, but the source of its failings generally seems to be in the politics, the imagination and the structure of local government. It is there, I think, that we now need the chief efforts of our critics.

The City as Environment

· KEVIN LYNCH

If the world were covered with a single vast city, how would one achieve the felicitous contrasts of city and country? The metaphor dramatizes the need for making the texture of great cities richer.

Imagine that the growth of population and the evolution of technology have urbanized the entire globe—that a single world city covers the usable surface of the earth. The prospect is a nightmare. One instantly has a vision of being trapped in endless rows of tenements or little suburban houses, of no escape from the continual presence and pressure of other people. The city would be monotonous, faceless, bewildering. It would be abstract, out of contact with nature; even the man-made things could not be handled or changed. The air would be foul, the water murky, the streets crowded and dangerous. Billboards and loudspeakers would force their attentions on everyone. One could be at home in a sealed room, but how could one farm or hunt or explore? Where could one find a wilderness or start a revolution? Would there be anything to challenge or excite the human spirit? Would not this world, entirely man-made, be utterly alien to every man? Surely it would be a vulnerable place: any shift of conditions would sweep it all away.

As a prediction of the quality of life in a world city these fears may be wildly irrational. We magnify the city we know, and this is what horrifies us. Our fright is too quick to be based on reasoning—even indirect reasoning. Cities have many human implications, and the studies in this book consider a number of them: history, economics, physical and social organization, problems of communication, transportation, land use and so on. Our fears, however, rise from another quarter: the way in which the environment affects our lives through our immediate perception and daily use of it. The physical form of a city has a sensuous impact that profoundly conditions the lives of its people, and this is often ignored in the task of city-building. By attempting, in our imagination, to make a world city habitable, we may discover policies that could harmonize the real metropolis.

The cities we live in have many admirable features, at least in the affluent, highly developed countries. The incidence of disease is low and the material standard of living higher than it has ever been in mankind's history. The modern metropolis provides unprecedented opportunities for education and entertainment. For millions of people it offers new ways of life that seem far more attractive to them than the old ones from which they are breaking away. Nonetheless, the metropolis has begotten problems that are monumental and notorious. Many of these are social and economic problems, but not the least of them is the harsh and confusing physical environment that has been created, which in itself aggravates social and personal problems.

Imagine, then, that we have been required to develop a sector of the hypothetical world city and to ameliorate as best we can the conditions it sets for the quality of life. What could we do to make it a more human place? What physical deficiencies make the great metropolises we know less than satisfying as places in which to live? There are perhaps four faults that stand out most sharply.

First and most obvious is the burden of perceptual stress imposed by the city. In particular we suffer from omnipresent noise (symbolic as well as acoustic) and an uncomfortable climate, including polluted air. The city is too hot, too noisy, too confusing:

the air is unpleasant to breathe. Too often the sensations we experience go beyond our limits of comfort or even of tolerance.

The second fault is a lack of visible identity. A good environment is richly diverse: its parts have distinct, identifiable character; they are marked by visible differences that allow choice and sensuous exploration, and they give a sense of place and home. A city is inherently a much richer and more diverse habitat than most rural areas, but it rarely appears to be so. Objective differences of activity, history and culture are glossed over and submerged. Large areas are zoned for similar land occupancy, which tends to separate different populations in a coarse grain. The physical setting could be managed to express and allow human diversity, and to bring those differences within sight of each other. We sense that the world city would be a trap because we are now trapped in a monotone city.

A third source of distress in our cities is their illegibility. In order to feel at home and to function easily we must be able to read the environment as a system of signs. It should be possible to relate one part to another and to ourselves, to locate these parts in time and space, and to understand their function, the activities they contain and the social position of their users. When the parts of the city lack visible relation to one another, their incoherence can contribute to a sense of alienation—of being lost in an environment with which one cannot carry on any sort of dialogue. Our cities display many ambiguities, confusions and discontinuities; significant activities are hidden from sight; history and natural setting are obscured. The language of the cityscape is as baffling as a news release.

The fourth disability of the city is its rigidity, its lack of openness. For his satisfaction and growth an individual needs opportunities to engage in active interchange with his environment: to use it, change it, organize it, even destroy it. His physical surroundings should be accessible and open-ended, challenging, wayward, responsive to effort. Individual action is a road to personal growth; cooperative action leads to satisfying interpersonal relations. These require a plastic physical setting, with opportunities for seclusion and for risk, and with a degree of ambiguity and waste. Woods, water and lonely places work this way, but so do empty buildings, back alleys, waste heaps, vegetable gardens, pits, caves and construction sites. They are not usually regarded as being beautiful, but this is a narrow view. They are the physical basis of an open society.

What might be done to correct these ills: discomfort, lack of diversity, illegibility, rigidity?

Discomfort must be attacked by taking the measure of the noxious sources and applying technology to control them. These questions have been scandalously neglected by the technological establishment of the advanced countries, hyperactive as it is in many other fields. We still lack detailed, quantitative knowledge about noise and pollution levels and human tolerances to them. In no large city has there been a systematic mapping of even the clearly definable qualities, such as the variations in microclimate, lighting or noise level. We will want to go further than suppression, to consider the possibilities for diversity and a stimulating rhythm of change. A universal hush or eternally mild sunny weather would be equally deadening.

In dealing with the other physical problems of the city (diversity, legibility, openness) I would concentrate to begin with on the character of the urban centers. These peaks of activity and interest, which dominate the urban scene because of their symbolic importance and the frequency with which they are occupied and seen, are the meeting ground for the diverse population of the metropolis, and they give character to large areas around themselves. They stand for the quality of the whole, and they act as foci for organization and memory. It would be my policy to sharpen whatever is unique in the physical character of each center and to increase the diversity between centers. Studies would be made of their existing differences and of their hidden potentialities—studies of each center's history, landform, building type, population and mix of activities. A program for visible character could be set for each focus, dealing with such qualities as the nature of exterior spaces, of lighting, planting and even the texture of the pavements. Each center could have an identifying focal point: a plaza, a crossroads, a terrace or a public room. The entrances to each center would be clarified, and its presence would be made visible from a distance. For the symbolic effect of contrast and for relief from the intensity of the central activities, I would take care to locate each center next to some natural feature: a rocky hill, a broad lake, a hidden stream, a tranquil garden.

High-intensity uses are currently moving outward from the central area to follow the movement of population. Often these uses seize on random suburban locations where land happens to be available and cars can be parked. In the process we are losing social and visual meeting points and the functional advantages of supporting interactivity. Some retail uses are relocating in compact regional shopping centers, but these are visually isolated from their surroundings and very limited in their range of activities. At other locations more comprehensive centers are gradually developing, but in a piecemeal fashion. Elsewhere old foci are expiring. Old or new, centers everywhere are incoherent and repetitious. (How many American shopping centers can be distinguished from one another from their photographs?)

What is happening suggests a twofold program: conserving and building up the old centers (or helping them to die gracefully if that is inevitable) and encouraging in the outer areas the coalescence of new centers with a wide range of activity. My goal would be a city-wide system of differentiated, compact centers, each reinforced by high-density housing and new educational or recreational institutions. The centers would be stable in location, giving the city continuity in time, but they would be changeable in form, reflecting the city's flux of activities and aspirations. It would be policy to preserve historic symbols and to limit locational drift, but not to freeze the patterns of use, whether within or between centers. We need not be bound by the structure of the past. Shifts in use should be encouraged, surfaces should be scarred by past traces and premonitory signs. The daily rhythm of activity could be made visible, the landscape charged with communications. These centers are the stable focal points of stimulus and change; I would make them visibly so.

Although the land in built-up centers in the U.S. typically is privately owned, this does not preclude planned change. Much can be achieved by zoning and other regulations, by the design of streets, open spaces and other public facilities, by the public renewal of strategic sections, by the provision of land or access, and by other positive or negative inducements to private developers.

Moreover, there is room for the development of new centers in the outlying areas of our metropolitan regions by public or semipublic agencies. These new centers might also serve as reception areas for low-income or segregated families escaping from inner-city ghettos. The inner centers may be preferred places in which to introduce new types of housing or recreational activity.

Open space is more easily accepted as being of public concern than is the planning of city centers, but our range of ideas in dealing with this feature is extremely narrow. Public open space usually means an athletic field, a beach, a lawn with trees and shrubs, a woodland with trails and picnic areas, perhaps a central plaza. Many other kinds can easily be imagined: mazes, heaths, thickets, canyons, rooftops, caves, marshes, canals, undersea gardens, yards for certain hobbies. We should design for diversity, experiment with new types, open recreational choices, fit opportunities to the real diversity of city people and their values.

Thinking of an endless world city reminds us how important it is that much of this be truly open space, permitting freely chosen activity, allowing us to manipulate things and make our own mark. Hobby yards could be provided, or sites for temporary gardens or self-help buildings. In this sense a dirt pile, a junkyard or a waste lot may be preferable to a rose garden, unless the roses are your own. We might present opportunities for adventure, challenge, even for real risk, if adjusted to individual ability. There could be difficult rock climbs, or dense brush for games of war or hunting. For much of this we can look to the present wastelands of our cities: the vacant lots, abandoned buildings, tidal flats, swamps, dumps, fields of weed and scrub, odd bits of land. We see in them the unhappy sign of neglect and decay; they are in fact a magnificent resource for recreation.

Open lands should be distributed throughout the metropolis in a fine-grained pattern, in contrast with the active urban areas, producing a varied texture of dense and free. A secluded park or a quiet walk, immediately adjacent to a center or to compact housing, can be more valuable to the city dweller than a remote preserve. Five-acre lots and many areas colored green on the map—estates, institutions, reservations—are of little use for public recreation. I would even try to create urban analogues of wilderness, open to the public but secluded, difficult of access, lean in human symbols. Spaces might be opened up to display characteristic views of city elements, to lay bare geologic formations, to dramatize the weather and the sky. There could be opportunities for observing and interacting with other species, or for studying the ecology of the city, including its human ecology. Camps could provide for experiments in social roles or for the innovation of new life styles. We may find that a prime use for obsolete inner-city land is for such diverse activities of recreation and education. Going to the inner city, with its full complement of intense urban use and diverse open space, could become an even more widespread way of enjoying vacation time than it is today.

The character of the centers and of the open spaces are two aspects of the city that influence the quality of living. There is a third, no less important: the system of paths along which people move and from which they perceive their environment. This is their observation platform for seeing the city, their principal means of comprehending it. It is from the path network that the city dweller sees the relations among the city's parts, recognizes its organization, becomes familiar with its landmarks and develops a sense of being at home instead of lost in the city's immensity. Since communication and meeting are the fundamental functions of the modern city, it is appropriate that their physical facilities provide the best means of understanding it.

I would give each path an identifiable character and make the network memorable as a system of clear and coherent sequences. The views from the system would expose the city's major physical parts, its dominant functions and its principal social areas. They would reveal its most interesting activities, its historical points, its geology (as in a cut for a roadway), its local fauna (the road traverses a huge aviary). Signs of impending change would be displayed, or symbols of community cooperation, celebration or even conflict. The movement system would be used not only as the visual organizer of the city but also as a prime source of information.

Many new highways and transit lines will be built by public agencies in our metropolitan areas in the next 20 years. The alignments and details of these routes could easily be planned to make traveling a delight as well as a necessity. The sequence of activities, open spaces, motions and details experienced along the route could be managed for the aesthetic pleasure of the moving ob-server. Each road could be given a coherent form and the inter-sections with other paths made clear. Names and visible character might be used to differentiate various roads and to explain their directions and destinations. This is a new art form that could add immeasurable richness to city life.

I would press hard for a diversity of routes, vehicles and styles of movement. The network would offer a variety of sequences that might be played in many combinations. Some routes would be designed as pleasureways, planned more for the motion along them to be enjoyed than for the simple function of circulation. There would be direct lines for people in a hurry and slow, lei-surely journeys for people on tour; challenging roads that tested a driver's skill and safe, easy means of transport for the infirm. Independent networks would be built not only for rail and auto-mobile traffic but also for walking, bicycling, riding and move-ment by water. New modes of travel could be developed, for ex-ample an economical transit system for the low-density suburbs (where a person without a car is now immobilized), or a safe, easily controlled vehicle (locatable on call by radio) in which children might roam with the freedom they once had in rural areas or small towns. Innovations in the means of travel might well be a public planning function.

The kind of action I am urging is not confined to developing new methods for new roads. It applies also to our present streets and highways, which—unpleasant, illegible and dangerous as they are—will be with us for at least another generation. Much could be done to improve these roads, by opening attractive views and clos-ing ugly ones, by changing lighting and pavement textures, by adding interesting roadside detail, by planting, and by designing more informative and meaningful signs.

We need not look forward with gloom to the future of the city. None of these proposals depend on freezing the city as it is or turning it back to some imaginary golden past. Metropolitan growth and "scatteration" at low densities, which is an expression of overriding preference on the part of a great majority of our people, could be welcomed, not bemoaned. There is no inherent reason why life in a metropolis, however large the city, should be unpleasant or restrictive, why it cannot be a satisfactory ground for human survival and development, why its people should be unable to look on it as a beloved landscape.

We cling to the notion of a world with an urban inside and a rural outside, divided between the exciting but dirty and disagreeable city and the placid countryside where people live in dull good health. The contrast is ceasing to have any validity. There have been artificial environments in the past that were cherished by their inhabitants with passionate attachment; most farm landscapes were of this kind. The sense of being at home does not depend on tidiness or tininess but on an active relation between men and their landscape, a pervasive meaningfulness in what they see. This meaningfulness is as possible in the city as in any other place, and probably more so.

For perhaps the first time in history we have the means of producing an enjoyable environment for everyone. It need not be saved for vacations but can be achieved in the world into which we wake every day. At the same moment we are becoming highly aware of the ugliness and discomfort the urban colossus now imposes on most of its inhabitants. Means and conscience should go together. Vast, drab and chaotic, the colossus looks permanent but is in fact changing rapidly. Its enormity, its complexity and changefulness, the diversity of function and life style, our scale of control in relation to the whole—all cause us to doubt our ability to manage the quality of our surroundings. Strategic action at the metropolitan scale is desperately needed. It is easy to criticize the city. What is not so obvious are its potentialities for satisfaction and delight, potentialities arising not just from the quality of the intimate setting—the house and its neighbors—but from the form of the city on the large scale. Although the quality of the local environment is also important, I have emphasized the large-scale possibilities since they are new and not so well known.

Our speculations on the problems of a world city have picked out at least three points of leverage for improving large-scale environmental quality: the movement system, the array of centers and the pattern of open spaces. We can imagine new possibilities for each of these, attractive directions for innovation in public policy. To this must be added the more traditional concerns for the adequacy and equity of housing and local services, the quality of site design, the control of noise, climate and the pollution of water and air. We could now begin to convert the real, existing metropolis into an environment in which men would take pride and pleasure. It could be made into something artificial in the old-fashioned sense of the word: a work of art, fitted to human purpose.

Bibliography

THE URBANIZATION OF THE HUMAN POPULATION

THE GROWTH OF CITIES IN THE NINETEENTH CENTURY: A STUDY IN STATISTICS. Adna Ferrin Weber. Columbia University, 1899.
URBAN RESEARCH METHODS. Edited by Jack P. Gibbs. D. Van Nostrand Company, Inc., 1961.
THE WORLD'S METROPOLITAN AREAS. University of California Press, 1959.

THE ORIGIN AND EVOLUTION OF CITIES

THE CITY IN HISTORY: ITS ORIGINS, ITS TRANSFORMATIONS, AND ITS PROSPECTS. Lewis Mumford. Harcourt, Brace & World, Inc., 1961.
CITY INVINCIBLE: A SYMPOSIUM ON URBANIZATION AND CULTURAL DEVELOPMENT IN THE ANCIENT NEAR EAST. Edited by Carl H. Kraeling and Robert M. Adams. The University of Chicago Press, 1960.
THE PREINDUSTRIAL CITY: PAST AND PRESENT. Gideon Sjoberg. The Free Press of Glencoe, Illinois, 1960.

THE MODERN METROPOLIS

THE CHANGING ECONOMIC FUNCTION OF THE CENTRAL CITY. Raymond Vernon. Committee for Economic Development, 1959.
THE ECONOMIC BASE OF THE METROPOLIS. Hans Blumenfeld in *Journal of the American Institute of Planners*, Vol. 21, No. 4, pages 114–132; 1955.
THE EXPLODING METROPOLIS. The editors of *Fortune*. Doubleday & Company, Inc., 1958.
THE STRUCTURE OF THE METROPOLITAN COMMUNITY: A STUDY OF DOMINANCE AND SUBDOMINANCE. Donald Joseph Bogue. University of Michigan, 1949.

THE TIDAL WAVE OF METROPOLITAN EXPANSION. Hans Blumenfeld in *Journal of the American Institute of Planners*, Vol. 20, No. 1, pages 3–14; Winter, 1954.

CALCUTTA: A PREMATURE METROPOLIS

CASTE AND OCCUPATION IN BHOWANIPUR, CALCUTTA. Anjana Roy Choudhury in *Man in India*, Vol. 44, No. 3, pages 207–220; July–September, 1964.

EASTERN INTERLUDE: A SOCIAL HISTORY OF THE EUROPEAN COMMUNITY IN CALCUTTA. H. Pearson. Thacker, Spink & Co. (1933), Ltd., 1954.

FIRST REPORT 1962. Calcutta Metropolitan Planning Organisation.

STOCKHOLM: A PLANNED CITY

SWEDISH SHOPPING CENTRES: EXPERIMENTS AND ACHIEVEMENTS. The Stockholm Chamber of Commerce, 1965.

ZONE EXPROPRIATION ON LOWER NORRMALM IN STOCKHOLM. E. G. Westman. Stockholm Regional and City Planning, 1964.

CIUDAD GUAYANA: A NEW CITY

THE BRITISH NEW TOWNS POLICY: PROBLEMS AND IMPLICATIONS. Lloyd Rodwin. Harvard University Press, 1956.

THE NEW TOWNS: THE ANSWER TO MEGALOPOLIS. Frederic J. Osborn and Arnold Whittick. Leonard Hill, 1963.

TOWARD NEW TOWNS FOR AMERICA. Clarence S. Stein. The University Press of Liverpool, 1951.

NEW YORK: A METROPOLITAN REGION

CITY AND SUBURB: THE ECONOMICS OF METROPOLITAN GROWTH. Edited by Benjamin Chinitz. Prentice-Hall, Inc., 1964.

1400 GOVERNMENTS: THE POLITICAL ECONOMY OF THE NEW YORK METROPOLITAN REGION. Robert C. Wood with Vladimir V. Almendinger, Harvard University Press, 1961.

METROPOLIS 1985: AN INTERPRETATION OF THE FINDINGS OF THE NEW YORK METROPOLITAN REGION STUDY. Raymond Vernon. Harvard University Press, 1960.

SPREAD CITY: PROJECTIONS OF DEVELOPMENT TRENDS AND THE ISSUES THEY POSE. THE TRI-STATE NEW YORK METROPOLITAN REGION, 1960–1985. Regional Plan Association, Inc., September, 1962.

The Uses of Land in Cities

Economics of Planned Development. Nathaniel Lichfield. The Estates Gazette, Ltd., 1956.

Land—A Special Issue. *House and Home*, August, 1960.

Land-Use Planning: A Casebook on the Use, Misuse, and Re-use of Urban Land. Charles M. Haar. Little, Brown and Company, 1959.

The Law of Open Space: Legal Aspects of Acquiring or Otherwise Preserving Open Space in the Tri-State New York Metropolitan Region. Shirley Adelson Siegel. Regional Plan Association, Inc., January, 1960.

Man's Struggle for Shelter in an Urbanizing World. Charles Abrams. The M.I.T. Press, 1964.

Revolution in Land. Charles Abrams. Harper & Row Publishers, 1939.

Transportation in Cities

An Analysis of Urban Travel Demands. Walter Y. Oi and Paul W. Shuldiner. Northwestern University Press, 1962.

Cities in the Motor Age. Wilfred Owen. The Viking Press, 1959.

Transportation and Urban Land. Lowdon Wingo, Jr. Resources for the Future, Inc., 1961.

Urban Transportation Planning: Concepts and Application. Highway Research Board Bulletin 293. National Academy of Sciences–National Research Council, 1961.

The Urban Transportation Problem. J. R. Meyer, J. F. Kain and M. Wohl. RAND Corporation and Harvard University Press, 1965.

The Metabolism of Cities

Environmental Change and Resulting Impacts on Health. World Health Organization Technical Report Series, No. 292; 1964.

Environmental Health Aspects of Metropolitan Planning and Development. World Health Organization Technical Report Series, No. 297; 1965.

The Future of Our Cities. Robert A. Futterman. Doubleday & Company, Inc., 1961.

Urban Atmospheric Pollution. Albert F. Bush in *Civil Engineering*, Vol. 35, No. 5, pages 66–68; May, 1965.

The Renewal of Cities

The Death and Life of Great American Cities. Jane Jacobs. Random House, 1961.

The Federal Bulldozer: A Critical Analysis of Urban Renewal, 1949–1962. Martin Anderson. The M.I.T. Press, 1964.

The Future of Old Neighborhoods: Rebuilding for a Changing Population. Bernard J. Frieden. The M.I.T. Press, 1964.

Planning and Politics: Citizen Participation in Urban Renewal. James Q. Wilson in *Journal of the American Institute of Planners*, Vol. 29, No. 4, pages 242–249; November, 1963.

The Social Implications of Urban Redevelopment. Peter Marris in *Journal of the American Institute of Planners*, Vol. 28, No. 3, pages 180–186; August, 1962.

The Urban Villagers: The Community Life of Italian-Americans. Herbert J. Gans. The Free Press, 1962.

The City as Environment

The Destruction of Britain? A Report on the Erosion of Our Countryside. Edward Hyams in *New Statesman*, pages 1005–1009; June 25, 1965.

The Image of the City. Kevin Lynch. The Technology Press & Harvard University Press, 1960.

Order in Diversity: Community without Propinquity. Melvin M. Webber in *Cities and Space: The Future Use of Urban Land*, edited by Lowdon Wingo, Jr. The Johns Hopkins Press, 1963.

The View from the Road. Donald Appleyard, Kevin Lynch and John R. Myer. The M.I.T. Press, 1964.

The Authors

KINGSLEY DAVIS ("The Urbanization of the Human Population") is professor of sociology and director of International Population and Urban Research at the University of California at Berkeley. He was born and reared in West Texas, then a highly rural region, where he acquired a strong preference for open spaces rather than cities. He was graduated from the University of Texas and received a master's degree in philosophy there; in 1936 he obtained a Ph.D. in sociology at Harvard University. Later he held a postdoctoral fellowship from the Social Science Research Council for advanced study in demography; more recently he was a fellow at the Center for Advanced Study in the Behavioral Sciences and a senior postdoctoral fellow of the National Science Foundation. His interest in population has taken him to Europe, Latin America, India, Pakistan and 10 countries in Africa; he has also served as U.S. representative to the Population Commission of the United Nations. Davis has been designated as chairman of the National Research Council's newly created Behavioral Sciences Division. Before going to the Oakland–San Francisco metropolitan area in 1955 he taught for seven years at Columbia University, a juxtaposition that moved him to write: "For a man who dislikes large cities, I have spent much of my adult life in major metropolitan areas."

GIDEON SJOBERG ("The Origin and Evolution of Cities") is associate professor of sociology at the University of Texas, where he has taught since 1949. He was graduated from the University of New Mexico in 1946, receiving a master's degree there a year later and a Ph.D. at the State College of Washington in 1949. He is the author of the book *The Preindustrial City: Past and Present*, and of numerous articles on urban sociology. From 1958 to 1964 he was a member of the Social Science Research Council's Committee on Urbanization.

HANS BLUMENFELD ("The Modern Metropolis") is a lecturer at the

School of Town and Regional Planning of the University of Toronto and planning consultant to several municipal and provincial agencies in Canada. He was born and educated in Germany. From 1921 to 1930 he practiced architecture there and in Austria and the U.S. He spent the next seven years in the U.S.S.R. working on city planning and architecture. He worked as a site planner in the New York area from 1938 to 1940, as a planning official and consultant in Philadelphia from 1941 to 1955 and as assistant director of the Metropolitan Toronto Planning Board from 1955 to 1961.

NIRMAL KUMAR BOSE ("Calcutta: A Premature Metropolis") is an anthropologist who was director of the Anthropological Survey of India for five years until 1964. He was born in the city of which he writes and was graduated from the University of Calcutta in 1921 with a degree in geology; later, after two years in Mahatma Gandhi's noncooperation movement, he returned to the university for graduate work in anthropology. He devoted many years to the movement for Indian independence and, like numerous other participants in the movement, spent some time in jail as a result of his activities. Periodically he taught anthropology and cultural geography at the University of Calcutta. Bose is the author of a number of books, several of them in English; the latter include *Cultural Anthropology* and *Studies in Gandhism*. For 15 years he has been editor of *Man in India*, the oldest anthropological journal in India. In 1961 and 1962 he conducted a survey on the urbanization of Calcutta; he is now engaged in writing the report.

GÖRAN SIDENBLADH ("Stockholm: A Planned City") is director of the Department of Planning and Building Control in Stockholm. He was born in Stockholm and was graduated in 1934 from the Royal Polytechnicum there as an architect. For 10 years he worked as a city planner in Stockholm and elsewhere and as a private consultant. In 1944 he joined the Stockholm Department of Planning to organize and work with the team that drew up a master plan for the city; the plan was published in 1952. Remaining with the department, he worked on suburban plans for three years before taking his present position. Sidenbladh has served on juries considering entries in planning competitions in Sweden, Germany, Denmark and Switzerland.

LLOYD RODWIN ("Ciudad Guayana: A New City") is chairman of the faculty committee of the Joint Center for Urban Studies of the Massachusetts Institute of Technology and Harvard University and professor in the department of city and regional planning at M.I.T.

He also serves as associate editor of *Daedaius*, the journal of the American Academy of Arts and Sciences. Rodwin, a native of New York City, was graduated from the City College of the City of New York in 1939 and received master's and doctor's degrees from Harvard University. He has been a member of the M.I.T. faculty since 1947. His activities include consulting work for many public and private organizations in the U.S. and abroad. He has written two books, *The British New Towns Policy* and *Housing and Economic Progress*, and now—during a year's leave of absence that he is spending abroad—is writing a book on national policies for urban and regional development. His chapter on Ciudad Guayana is a substantially revised version of a brochure on urban planning in developing areas that he prepared for the U.S. Housing and Home Finance Agency and the Agency for International Development.

BENJAMIN CHINITZ ("New York: A Metropolitan Region") is professor of economics and chairman of the department of economics at the University of Pittsburgh. He is also associate director of the university's Center for Regional Economic Studies. Chinitz was graduated from Yeshiva University in 1945 and received a master's degree from Brown University and a doctor's degree from Harvard University. He has taught at Dartmouth College and at Brown University. From 1956 to 1959 he was a senior member of the staff of the New York Metropolitan Region Study. His activities include work as a consultant for the President's Appalachian Regional Commission, the RAND Corporation and the Connecticut State Development Commission.

CHARLES ABRAMS ("The Uses of Land in Cities") is chairman of the city-planning department at Columbia University and director of the university's new Institute of Urban Environment. He is a lawyer who for many years has conducted in New York City a practice specializing in housing law. Born in Poland and brought to the U.S. as a child, he began his practice after obtaining a law degree from St. Lawrence University. In a career spanning more than 40 years he has served as a member of United Nations missions to several nations, as counsel to various city, state and Federal housing bodies and, from 1955 to 1959, as chairman of the New York State Commission against Discrimination. Abrams is the author of many books and articles arising from his professional activities. Having just completed a new book (*The City Is the Frontier*), he is at work writing a housing program for the Province of Quebec.

JOHN W. DYCKMAN ("Transportation in Cities") is chairman of the Center for Planning and Development Research and professor of city and regional planning at the University of California at Berkeley. In Chicago, his birthplace, he obtained a bachelor's degree in education from Chicago Teachers College in 1944, a master's degree in economics from the University of Chicago in 1951 and a Ph.D. in planning from the same institution in 1957. He was a member of the faculty of the city-planning department at the University of Pennsylvania for eight years and then became chief of the Regional Development and Urban Economic Section of Arthur D. Little, Inc., in San Francisco before going to the University of California. Dyckman has served as consultant to the National Park Service, the New York City Planning Department, the Planning Board of Puerto Rico, the American Council to Improve Our Neighborhoods (ACTION) during the formative stages of the program, and several other organizations.

ABEL WOLMAN ("The Metabolism of Cities") is emeritus professor of sanitary engineering at Johns Hopkins University and consulting engineer to many municipal, state, Federal and foreign agencies. He was born in Baltimore and was graduated from Baltimore City College in 1909, later taking degrees in arts and in engineering at Johns Hopkins. From 1915 to 1939 he was with the Maryland State Department of Health, first as an assistant engineer and—for 17 years—as chief engineer. He has also been editor or associate editor of several professional journals, among them the *American Journal of Public Health*, the *Journal of the American Water Works Association* and *Municipal Sanitation*. At various times he was a lecturer in sanitary engineering at Princeton University, the University of California at Berkeley, the University of Chicago and Johns Hopkins before assuming his professorship at Johns Hopkins in 1937. Among the many agencies for which Wolman was or is a consultant are the U.S. Public Health Service, the World Health Organization and the Tennessee Valley Authority. He has also been a consultant to a number of cities throughout the world, and for several years he was chairman of the board of consultants assembled by Israel for its Jordan River Project. He is currently serving as chairman of a panel on water resources for the U.S. Agency for International Development.

NATHAN GLAZER ("The Renewal of Cities") is professor of sociology at the University of California at Berkeley. Born in New York City, he was graduated from the City College of the City of New York in 1944; he received a master's degree from the University of

Pennsylvania and a doctor's degree from Columbia University. From 1944 to 1953 he was on the staff of *Commentary*, and he then spent several years as an editor or editorial adviser with book-publishing firms in New York. Glazer has also taught sociology at Bennington College and Smith College and spent a year as an urban sociologist with the Housing and Home Finance Agency in Washington. He is the author of *American Judaism* and *The Social Basis of American Communism*, coauthor (with David Riesman and Reuel Denney) of *The Lonely Crowd* and coauthor (with Riesman) of *Faces in the Crowd.*

KEVIN LYNCH ("The City as Environment") is professor of city planning at the Massachusetts Institute of Technology, with which he has been associated as a student and teacher since 1946. Before that he studied at Yale University's School of Architecture, at Taliesin, the late Frank Lloyd Wright's center for budding architects, and at the Rensselaer Polytechnic Institute. He has also spent, since 1940, a year in a Chicago architectural firm, five years in the U.S. Army, a year as assistant director of the department of city planning in Greensboro, N.C., and a year in Italy on a Ford Foundation fellowship. Lynch has been particularly interested in the form of cities: he has written several articles and books on the subject; he was codirector of a five-year Rockefeller Foundation research project on the perceptual form of the city, and he is at present engaged in studies of visual form at the metropolitan scale.

A Note on the Type

THE TEXT of this book was set on the Linotype in *Janson*, a recutting made direct from type cast from matrices long thought to have been made by the Dutchman ANTON JANSON, who was a practicing type founder in Leipzig during the years 1668-87. However, it has been conclusively demonstrated that these types are actually the work of Nicholas Kis (1650-1702), a Hungarian, who most probably learned his trade from the master Dutch type founder Dirk Voskins. The type is an excellent example of the influential and sturdy Dutch types that prevailed in England up to the time William Caslon developed his own incomparable designs from these Dutch faces.

Composed, printed, and bound by
H. Wolff, Inc., New York